1,001

GREAT

GIFTS

By
Jane A. Brody, Suzanne Gruber,
Regina McAloney, Ellen Scher
and Betsy Sheldon

CAREER PRESS
3 Tice Road
P.O. Box 687
Franklin Lakes, NJ 07417
1-800-CAREER-1
201-848-0310 (NJ and outside U.S.)
Fax: 201-848-1727

1,001 GREAT GIFTS

ISBN 1-56414-253-1, $12.99
Cover design by Dean Johnson Design, Inc.
Printed in the U.S.A. by Book-mart Press

To order this title by mail, please include price as noted above, $2.50 handling per order, and $1.00 for each book ordered. Send to: Career Press, Inc., 3 Tice Road, P.O. Box 687, Franklin Lakes, NJ 07417.

Or call toll-free 1-800-CAREER-1 (NJ and Canada: 201-848-0310) to order using VISA or MasterCard, or for further information on books from Career Press.

Library of Congress Cataloging-in-Publication Data

1,001 great gifts / by Jane A. Brody ... [et al.].
    p. cm.
   ISBN 1-56414-253-1 (pbk.)
   1. Gifts. I. Brody, Jane A.
GT3050.A159 1996
   394--dc20   96-23342
                                                             CIP

Dedication

To our friends and family, in recognition of the many gifts *you've* given *us*, especially the ones that could not be listed in a book—time, attention and love.

Acknowledgments

We would like to thank all of the people we pestered for gift ideas as the deadline for our manuscript approached. Your valuable suggestions and your true stories of gift-giving experiences, both successful and embarrassing, made this book much more than a mere gift list.

We would also like to thank our editor, Gloria Fuzia, for giving us a fresh perspective. Who knows what might have happened if you had allowed us to keep that thong underwear idea in the parents section!

Contents

1,001 Great Gifts

If you've been kicked by the gift horse one time too many

One of the authors of this book, let's call her Doris,* remembered as she left for a family reunion that it was a sister-in-law's birthday. She rummaged through a closet of picture frames, stationery boxes and other assorted emergency gift items and selected a ceramic candleholder. As her sister-in-law pulled the gift from its tissue-wrapped bag, Doris recalled—too late—that not only had her sister-in-law given her the candleholder on a previous holiday, she had also given it the same gift bag that Doris had saved for reuse!

Another author—let's call this one Stella*—once searched and searched for the perfect gift for a music-loving friend. She finally found a lovely pair of earrings—large silver treble clefs decorated in colorful enamel dangling from coiled, pierced hoops. Expensive, but worth it for her eccentric friend who, as it turned out, did *not* have pierced ears.

Yet another author, Ethel* this time, recalls a co-worker revealing that he yearned to have a dog. For the man's birthday, Ethel was delighted to surprise her associate with a puppy she'd saved from the animal shelter. What Ethel quickly discovered, as the man began sneezing, was the reason he didn't *have* a dog—he was extremely allergic to animals.

There's no doubt about it: Gift-giving is one of the most daunting challenges facing anyone—even for those who dare to write books on the subject. We keep reading that speaking in public is the greatest fear

---

* Names have been changed to protect the guilty.

of most people—even greater than the fear of death. We don't believe this to be true. According to *our* research, these are the top fears (in no particular order) of the American public:

- The fear of holiday gift exchanges at the office.

- The fear that the deluxe-model julienne zucchini slicer you bought for your best friend's birthday is the same gift you gave her last year.

- The fear of giving your dad one more tie that—you suspect— he only pulls out of the box to wear when *you* come over so you won't ever know that he wouldn't be caught dead outside the house in it.

- The fear that your teenage nephew will roll his eyes behind your back after opening the CD you gave him.

- The fear that your friend's toddler will prefer the paper and the bow to the gift that you'd wrapped inside.

- The fear that you will forget about Christmas, Chanukah, Valentine's Day, Mother's Day or some other major gift-giving holiday—until midnight before the big day.

This book is for the phobic gift-giver, the dysfunctional shopper, the generosity-challenged, the decision-impaired. It is the answer for those individuals who, for whatever reason, cringe at the coming of Christmas, not to mention birthdays and such Hallmark-inspired holidays as Secretary's Day and Grandparents' Day.

In this book are hundreds of gift ideas for such individuals. And not just traditional or practical gifts. We include the daring and the one-of-a-kind. We offer the inexpensive and the homemade. We present the outrageous and the all-out-splurges. We feature the unbeatable and the unforgettable. In short, there's something for *everyone*. And that includes:

- Parents—your parents, other people's parents, people you *wish* were your parents, your grandparents, aunts, uncles and mentors.

- Children—your own, nieces and nephews, grandchildren, friends' children, babies, toddlers and school-aged children.

- Teenagers—yours or those related to you, baby sitters, teenagers who drive cars and teenagers going to college.

- Significant others—first-dates, serious squeezes, fiancés, live-in loves, new spouses and spouses you've hung onto for half a century or more.

- Friends—casual friends, lifelong friends, new friends, friends getting married, friends buying homes, friends expecting babies or friends expecting you for dinner.

- Co-workers—associates, cubicle mates, rivals, bosses, assistants, vendors, clients and networking contacts.

- And others—animal lovers, gourmets, travelers, collectors, sports lovers, couch potatoes and anyone else you may possibly have to buy a gift for.

You'll notice that this book isn't organized by gift-giving occasion, say Christmas or Mother's Day or even birthdays. Truth is, you'd buy your sister the same sweater for Christmas as you would for her birthday. Instead, the book is organized by recipient. Because that's what poses the most problems for gift-givers. What do I give a *parent* who already has everything she wants? What kind of music do I buy for a *16-year-old* who wears baggy pants and has a pierced nose?

Each chapter includes anecdotes (our recommendations are tried-and-true!) and gift ideas for special occasions or situations. For example, in Chapter 3, on teenagers, we offer ideas for bar and bat mitzvahs and religious confirmations. Chapter 6, on friends, features suggestions for housewarming gifts, baby shower gifts, hostess gifts and lots more.

Indeed, we offer 1,001 great gift ideas. However, in a given chapter, not *every* gift is great for *every* person. Gift-giving and garage sales share a common theme: "One person's trash is another person's treasure." Thus, the dad who'd cherish a silver, engraved business card holder is not necessarily the same dad who'd appreciate a Three Stooges tie. And the friend who'd value a few shares of stock may not place the same value on a book about astrology. But we assure you of this: Each chapter of this book *will* contain dozens of gift possibilities for even the hardest-to-buy-for.

In addition, we identify for your convenience which gifts may best meet (or be excluded from) your personal criteria or limitations—say, for example, you're on a budget, or you're looking for a really unusual idea. We indicate these gifts with a special symbol that appears to the left of the listing. Look for these classifications:

Expensive
($100 or more)

Homemade

Inexpensive
($10 or less)

Far out/unusual

Sentimental

These classifications are, of course, somewhat objective. For example, although we classify an astrological reading of your friend's new-born baby "far out," we're sure there are some people who practically live by astrology and wouldn't view this gift as anything out of the ordinary. Further, our "expensive" and "inexpensive" classifications are meant only as general guidelines. For example, we deem earrings for a teenager "inexpensive," but detailed, designer, 14k-gold hoops will obviously cost more than a simple pair of trendy, stainless-steel studs.

1,001 Great Gifts—in addition to its gift listings—offers much more. Chapter 1 features great tips for planning ahead for gift-giving occasions. By utilizing a gift calendar, keeping gift profiles, stocking a supply of our recommended "on-hand" gifts and preparing last-minute gift strategies, you should never have to confront the last fear listed on page 10—the fear of forgetting to get a gift for an important occasion—again! And finally, we give you some great suggestions for gift presentation in Chapter 9.

We admit it: We have made our share of gift-giving blunders. But we hope through our collective experiences and our efforts to gather for you some of the most unique, creative, romantic, clever, thoughtful, cool, practical, outrageous, traditional, radical, one-of-a-kind and cherished gifts—you will benefit from *our* mistakes and become the person to whom all your friends, family and acquaintances will exclaim, "You always know the perfect gift to give!" And if everything else fails, you can always give the recipient a copy of this book. Trust us—they'll love it.

Chapter 1

Planning ahead takes the stress out of gift-giving

Gift-giving is difficult for many reasons: budget constraints, uncertainty about what to give, the desire to get just the right thing. But what *really* aggravates the situation more than any other factor? Procrastination! Christmas is two days away, the malls are packed and you haven't *begun* to shop... You're on your way to the folks' to celebrate Mother's Day and pray there's a drugstore open in their neighborhood so you can pick up a bottle of perfume... You have to run out during lunch to pick up a card for the co-worker who's cake break is planned at 1 p.m.

How to overcome this stress? Same way you confront it at work, with household chores, with budgeting and anything else—you have to plan ahead! By setting aside a small amount of time—just a few minutes, really—you can give some thought to the individual you're buying for, identify personal preferences or interests, list some great gift possibilities, schedule a shopping trip and have the whole thing wrapped up in plenty of time for the big occasion.

While not quite a 12-step program, we offer the following strategies to help you overcome gift-giving procrastination.

1. Schedule it

Buy (or make) yourself a special calendar or datebook devoted to all gift-giving occasions. (We have also supplied one for you in Appendix 3, pages 152 to 163.) Be sure it's a perpetual calendar, one not restricted to a single year, so you can keep it forever. Write in all the birthdays, anniversaries, holidays and special gift-giving dates for family, friends and everyone you'd give a gift to. As time goes on, you can continue to add new friends and new occasions as they come up.

Wait! You're not done yet. Now, from each gift-giving occasion, backtrack about two weeks and write in reminders for shopping and card-buying trips. Or if you keep a separate day planner or "to-do" calendar, memo yourself there to shop for the gift. This way, you don't run the risk of turning the calendar page to discover that *today* is Great-aunt Thelma's birthday and you're tied up in meetings 'til midnight.

2. Keep a gift profile

Capture the relevant information about the family and friends on your gift list—clothing sizes, favorite hobbies, birthstones, etc. This will leave room in your memory for matters more pressing than your Uncle Arnold's waist size. It'll also save you the trouble of asking the same person his or her favorite color until *you're* blue in the face!

Easy-to-use, fill-in-the-blank gift-giving profiles are also included in Appendix 3 on pages 164 and 165. Photocopy and add them to your gift calendar, and you have all the relevant information you need to be a gift-giver extraordinaire! Well, almost.

3. Track your gift history

As part of that gift profile, you'll want to keep a history of gifts you've given to that individual. (See page 166.) This will prevent you from giving a similar item two years in a row. You can even add comments regarding reactions to the gifts, if you found them noteworthy. (For example: "Jumped up and down with joy," "Started sneezing as soon as she wrapped the feather boa around her neck.")

4. Keep gift items on hand

Even with all of these advance-planning and organizational techniques, you just might forget a particular occasion or be invited somewhere last-minute, and you'll need a gift...quick! Here are some items you can keep on hand—items that will be suitable as gifts for just about any occasion, from graduation get-togethers to retirement receptions to grab-bag gatherings.

1. **Stationery or note cards.** Have a variety on hand. Stationery is a great solution for your kids' teachers as well as hostess gifts.

2. **Fine chocolates.** People generally receive chocolates enthusiastically, especially "designer" brands. Stock up when you see a sale. They'll last indefinitely in the freezer.

3. **Picture frames.** Keep several in various styles and sizes. Almost everybody loves photos—whether to show off grandchildren or the event for which you're giving the gift.

4. **Photo albums.** Ditto.

5. **Wallets.** Appreciated by almost anyone, these essentials never go out of style if you choose a basic leather version. Buy several when you see a sale.

6. **Movie tickets or certificate books.** These can often be ordered at a discount from organizations like AAA, or national dining out and entertainment discount clubs such as Transmedia.

7. **Bath items.** Sample-size bath and shower gels, scented lotions, shampoos and powders gathered in a tiny basket or net bag are available for women, men and children. You can find them prepackaged for reasonable prices at specialty shops such as The Body Shop—but they're often available at discount department stores as well.

8. **Wines, liqueurs and other alcoholic beverages.** A nice bottle of wine is an ideal gift for most occasions—birthdays, anniversaries, promotions or the celebration of any good fortune—and a good wine doesn't have to set you back a lot. The other advantage is that you can stock up when you find a good buy and be assured that it won't go bad if you keep it around for a while! Depending upon the recipient's taste, you might consider, instead, a flavored liqueur or an aged Scotch. But whatever you choose, make sure that the individual doesn't have any religious or personal objections to alcohol.

5. Shop with savvy

Whether you're shopping for stock-up gifts or buying ahead as scheduled in your gift calendar, you can take a few additional steps to enhance your gift-selection success.

- Shop with a shopper. We all know a handful of people who indeed seem to have been born to shop. They have an inborn radar for great buys and good quality—and an instinct for matching gifts to recipients. So if you choke at the prospect of surfing the mall, offer to buy lunch for your favorite shopaholic and tap into his or her expertise.

- Shop with someone who fits the "profile" of your gift recipient when possible. Buying for a teenage girl? Hire your baby sitter for an afternoon at the mall. Looking for a birthday gift for your sports-nut brother? Ask your buddy at work to sacrifice a lunch hour for a shopping trip. And if they can't come shopping with you, probe them about the kinds of gifts *they'd* appreciate most.

- Even if you end up shopping alone, chances are you'll have a successful trip if you do your homework ahead of time. This means making a list of a few potential gift items (not too many), calling stores ahead of time to see if they carry the items and then targeting just a few stores that you know will have what you're looking for. Wandering into a multilevel mall without a game plan can result in waves of anxiety for the shopping dysfunctional.

- Buy from mail-order catalogs. To eliminate the stress and effort of *going* shopping, keep a handful of those pesky catalogs that fill your mailbox—even if you don't regularly order from them. Flip through them when they arrive, and mark with sticky notes the items you think others might appreciate. Then, when a birthday or other gift-giving occasion is on the horizon, simply call and order. Most catalog companies will deliver to the recipient and include a message. For a listing of just a few of these catalogs, see Appendix 1 beginning on page 141.

6. Other tips, tricks and gift-giving strategies

If your primary struggle with gift-giving is identifying what to give, the simplest solution is to ask the individual. Oh, sure, you'll run into the uncooperative parent who claims he or she doesn't need anything but your company, but most people *will* provide you with some clues. Children will eagerly describe the cool new toy they saw advertised on Saturday morning cartoons. Brides and grooms will gladly refer you to their registry, and teenagers will likely even give you price, make and model number of the latest high-tech gizmo they're coveting.

The next-best strategy is to ask a close friend or relative for ideas—the bride's best friend, the child's mother, the boss's assistant, the boyfriend's brother. In fact, this might even be a superior strategy if you're dealing with a modest soul who's uncomfortable with "asking" for things. Friend Norma insists the only thing she wants for her 50th birthday is all her friends to be with her. Husband Bob reveals that Norma's been dreaming of a beauty makeover with massage and manicure at the local spa.

7. Last-minute tactics

You're on your way to someone's celebration and you don't have a gift? Run to the drugstore and select a magazine you know the individual would enjoy reading. Make sure as you pick it up that you don't lose all those annoying "blow-in" subscription cards—you're going to fill in the name and address of the celebrant on one of them, indicate that you should be billed (be sure to include *your* address in the proper spot) and drop it in the mail. *Voilà!* You've solved your gift emergency! You arrive bearing a gift that will keep on giving! Simply present your package and explain that the next issue will be arriving at the recipient's address in a few weeks.

If you have a *little* more time—say, a day or so—call a gift basket service. Most cities have several listed in the yellow pages. You can typically select colors and contents depending upon the individual and occasion. Such baskets are often filled with gourmet food items (coffees and special cookies) or bath items (lotions, scrubs and shower gels) or a combination. One gift-basket service in the Midwest puts together a basket for newlyweds that includes a bottle of champagne with two glasses, a few food items and a bronze door knocker. (Give them an extra day and they'll have it engraved!) Baskets can be pricey; the most basic running $25 or so and increasing in price depending upon the contents. Most services will put together a customized gift and deliver it often within a day of ordering, and these gifts never fail to rate high on the "ooh and ahhh" scale.

Something for everyone

Once you've followed the strategies laid out in this chapter, procrastination should never again plague your gift-giving activity. Yet you still may struggle with new and creative gift ideas for the numerous occasions that demand your generosity. The rest of this book is devoted to such ideas—*hundreds* of ideas—compiled to solve your gift-giving bewilderment for good.

Chapter 2

Presents to please even the pickiest parents

L et's face it—parents are some of the toughest people to buy for. First, they're older, so they've known exactly what they want—and don't want—for longer. Plus, they have a habit of immediately buying whatever it is they want. To aggravate the situation further, they never give us any help at all—when we ask them for gift-giving guidance, they typically reply, "Oh, nothing, dear. Just knowing you're happy and healthy is all the gift I need."

To make matters worse, with anniversaries and other joint gift-giving occasions, we have to contend with their conflicting tastes and preferences. So you think a CD is a safe gift for the both of them? Mom loves classical, Dad only listens to jazz. Maybe tickets to an event? Mom's big on ballet, Dad's a hockey fan.

Your folks may be picky. Or perhaps their health problems limit your range of gift possibilities. Or maybe the problem isn't just with your parents, but other members of your family as well. Maybe it's tradition to chip in with your siblings—but your brother the doctor wants to send the folks on a Caribbean cruise while your sister the starving artist was thinking along the lines of a massaging shower head.

Considering these scenarios and countless others, it's easy to see why you bought this book. While we certainly can't resolve all of these challenges (we can think of no adequate compromise between a Caribbean cruise and a massaging shower head), we've provided you with 146 great ideas to consider for your parents' birthdays, Christmas or

Chanukah, anniversary, Mother's Day, Father's Day, retirement—or any other gift-giving occasion that tests your mettle as a devoted son or daughter.

Note that the gifts in this chapter don't apply strictly to your mother and father. They can be considered for your in-laws, your grandparents, your 96-year-old Aunt Shirley, your Bohemian academic mentor—and any relative or individual who's got some seniority on you.

1. An authentic day-you-were-born newspaper—often presented in an attractive portfolio. These can be purchased from some mail-order companies.

2. A gift certificate to a restaurant. You can send Mom and Dad to a tried-and-true place they love or to one they've always wanted try.

3. Ballroom dancing lessons. Helps keep the spirit of fun and romance alive.

4. His-and-hers watches.

5. A customized calendar featuring photos of your family each month of the year. Kinko's Copies, as well as several mail-order companies, makes these.

 A golf course membership and lessons. A relaxing way to spend free time.

7. A pair of sturdy athletic shoes. Cross-trainers are appropriate— Mom or Dad may use them for anything from yoga to running to self-defense class.

8. Matching jogging suits—even if they'll only wear them to the mall together.

 An artist's rendering of your parents' home on a plate, wall plaque, canvas, etc.

10. A horse-drawn carriage ride. Treat Mom and Dad to this romantic journey in a large city.

For promoting good health

Older adults are healthier and more active than ever. It's likely your parents are involved in some sort of fitness program—whether mall-walking or rock-climbing. And they're probably more watchful of their diet than they were as young adults. Show your support by giving gifts that support a healthy lifestyle. Here are a few suggestions:

 A membership to a fitness center—for a few months, a year or longer. Look for clubs that offer components you know they'll enjoy, such as massages, a steam room, a pool, special classes for older adults, etc.

12. A seat cushion (it looks like a car seat cushion) that is actually a soothing, vibrating massager. It comes with a control panel that allows you to adjust speed, areas of your back or legs to massage and intensity of vibrations. Sold by Brookstone (see Appendix 1).

13. Chiropractic sessions if Mom or Dad has been complaining about neck, shoulder or back pain.

14. A showerhead with massaging powers (Teledyne Water Pik offers a great one) can make for a relaxing or invigorating shower.

15. A carbon monoxide detector.

16. A water cooler and spring water. Good for drinking and cooking and, in some locations, a healthier alternative to tap water. You can rent the cooler and purchase the water from a company such as Poland Spring (800-759-9251).

17. A water filter that attaches to a tap or is placed over a pitcher.

18. A cool mist humidifier.

For promoting good health

19. A blood pressure monitor can be purchased at department stores, through catalogs, etc. This way, your folks can monitor their blood pressure and stress level.

20. A juicer. Some swear that "juicing" fruits and vegetables puts all the vitamins straight to work.
     Robert and his sister Terri bought one for their parents for the holidays because their father is on a restricted diet. Now he makes his own juice and enjoys it, knowing that it's 100-percent healthy for him.

21. A special-diet cookbook. If one or both parents is on a special diet, buy a few books appropriate to their needs. You can pique their interest in the contents by cooking a special meal from one.

22. A vegetable steamer and a cookbook on high-vitamin cooking.

23. *The Pill Book, The Doctor's Book of Home Remedies* or *The Bantam Medical Dictionary*, all published by Bantam. Your folks can learn about commonly prescribed drugs, techniques for everyday health problems and illnesses.

24. *Alternative Healing* by Arnold and Barry Fox. It discusses home remedies and other alternative therapies for health problems ranging from arthritis to ulcers.

25. A whirlpool foot massager/bath.

26. Decaffeinated coffee beans and a bean grinder.

27. An electronic diet and nutrition guide—displays nutritional facts (calories, fat, cholesterol, sodium) for thousands of foods.

28. Season tickets to a favorite pastime—anything from hometown football to the opera.

 For parents who have a closet full of slides or eight-millimeter home movies with an obsolete film projector, put their old pictures and/or movies on videotape. You can pay by the foot to have this done by a professional (which could cost hundreds of dollars), rent the transfer equipment or buy it for as little as $40. Effects and sound can be added to make an even more exciting presentation.

30. A gift certificate for a portrait session—with just Mom and Dad, or including kids and grandkids—and a set of prints.

 A set of matching recliners. Costly, yes, but it makes a great joint gift among siblings.

32. A Transmedia, Entertainment or other discount book for the local area that offers savings as high as 50 percent on dining out, amusements, shopping, travel, etc. Call 800-422-5090 for Transmedia.

33. Coffee-table books. Try a big, glossy picture book about a place that's special to them or one about a destination they've always wanted to visit.

 A closet organizing system, such as one from the California Closet Company. It only takes a few hours to set it up, and if you let your parents know beforehand, you can have it done while they are not home. One Rockland County, N.Y., company charges $269, installation included.

35. Books on tape. Great for traveling or working around the house, and a lot easier on the eyes.

36. Unless they're nondrinkers, give Mom and Dad a vintage wine, aged Scotch or a special liqueur they're likely to savor.

For the older parent

As our parents age, we develop more concern for their safety and physical limitations. They (and we) may not like it, but they're going through physical and emotional changes, and these changes need to be accommodated. We can help to make their lives easier and more pleasant with the gifts we give.

 A landscaping/maintenance service for property allows your parents to relax instead of pulling weeds on hot, humid days.

38. A "pen steadier"—a plastic stand that holds a pen firmly to give those with shaky hands more control over their handwriting. Sold in the Miles Kimball catalog. (See Appendix 1 for more information on this mail-order company.)

39. A magazine subscription in large-type format. *Reader's Digest*, for example, offers this easy-on-the-eyes option.

40. Large-print books. The classics and not-so-classics can be purchased in this form. Inquire at a bookstore.

41. A fold-up shopping cart with wheels to make transporting groceries easier.

 A greeting card assortment and stamps so they don't have to go out and buy a new card for every celebration of family and friends.

43. Membership to American Association of Retired Persons (AARP). This organization costs about $8 per year per couple, but you can purchase a three-year membership for $20 and a 10-year membership for $45. Membership includes the *AARP Bulletin, Modern Maturity* magazine, educational publications, special insurance and travel rates, pharmacy service savings and more. For an extra fee, you can add a 24-hour roadside service plan. Call 800-424-3410.

For the older parent

44. A laundry chute installed on an upper level of the home, so they don't have to collect laundry from all over the house and carry it down the stairs.

45. A rocking chair. Yes, it's cliché, but that's not necessarily a bad thing. To boost its authenticity, place it on the porch if possible.

46. A watch with large, easy-to-read numbers.

47. A telephone with large numbers.

48. A magnifying glass is a useful gift for reading maps, mail, etc. You can get one that is strictly functional or one that can be displayed to add beauty to the home.

 A housecleaning service on a regular basis can be a great help. Mom and Dad can always supervise, but they don't have to use their own elbow grease.

50. Hire a chiropodist to come to the house and cut his or her toenails. As people get older, it's not so easy for them to stretch.

51. A gift certificate for a seamstress or tailor to save them the time it takes to make repairs, especially if eyesight is poor.

52. A walking stick that converts to a three-legged stool. Check in one of those sophisticated gadget catalogs or shops, such as Brookstone (see Appendix 1).

53. A bathtub seat for those who need to sit down while showering.

 Birthday greetings from the White House. Once your loved one reaches a certain age, write to the President and he will send a birthday message.

For the older parent

 Willard Scott's 100th-birthday (for the centenarian) or 75th-anniversary greeting on the *Today* show. Write to Willard Scott's 100th Birthday Greetings, 30 Rockefeller Plaza, Room 352, New York, NY 10112. Send the name and address of the celebrant and a photo (which will not be returned) three to four weeks in advance of the intended air date, and include your daytime phone number so you can be reached for the details.

56. Bathroom grab bars and bathtub floor appliqués for those with unsteady footing.

57. Houseslippers and a bathrobe. Add a monogram for a personal touch.

 Send fresh-cut flowers every week or every other week to keep the environment cheery. Call 800-836-PETAL for information.

59. A cordless phone. Especially good for the parent living alone, who can't tell someone else to get the phone if he or she is in the bath. If possible, get a model with a volume control button.

60. A garbage can on wheels.

61. A subscription to *Choice Magazine Listening*. This is a free service that provides excerpts from well-known publications to those with visual or physical impairments. A special tape player is provided free from the Library of Congress. Call 516-883-8280 for more information.

62. Flannel sheets.

63. Binoculars. For concerts, bird-watching, horse races, etc.

Grandparenthood

When your parents become grandparents, their perspective changes. Crying infants in restaurants sound like songbirds, wet fingerprints on mirrors are masterpieces. Give them something to celebrate a birth in the family or commemorate their role on Grandparents' Day.

64. New grandfather: a watch with baby's birthstone. A masculine piece of jewelry with sentiment to remind him of the new addition to the family.

65. New grandmother: Any jewelry with baby's birthstone to remind her of her new grandchild.

66. Subscription to *Reminisce*, a nostalgia magazine, to put them back in touch with their youth.

 Pictures of children and grandchildren. Whether it's a "glamour shot" of a favorite granddaughter, one of those dress-up "vintage" photos of the whole family in saloon attire or a set of school pictures, they're sure to be appreciated and shared.

68. A grandfather clock, of course. What better time (pun intended) to buy one? These are also available in miniatures.

 Baseball caps, T-shirts, coffee mugs, mouse pads and many other items can have photos of grandchildren transferred onto them.

70. A weekend at a cozy bed-and-breakfast or a resort. Buy them an all-inclusive package so everything is taken care of for them, from a welcome fruit basket to breakfast in bed.

 A big-screen TV with surround-sound.

Wedding anniversary

Wedding anniversaries may be trying occasions to purchase for because you must buy a joint gift that will please both parents. Home improvement gifts are ideal, especially if they somehow commemorate the special occasion.

 A patchwork quilt made with patches of fabric painted, designed or decorated and signed by those in the immediate family, including all the grandkids. Serves as a functional "family tree" that will keep Mom and Dad warm.

73. A silver platter, engraved with the date and their names. Include a container of silver polish.

74. A Lenox plate that can be displayed serves as a tangible and beautiful reminder of the special day.

 Present them with a list of every good thing they've done for you since birth. Have a calligrapher write it out on a framable piece of stationery. End it with a huge "Thanks." (Mom and Dad always love to be reminded of all they've done for you...so spell it out for them!)

76. Have a sketch or painting of them done by a professional artist. You can give the artist a snapshot to copy from.

 Send your parents on a memorable trip.
For her parents' 50th anniversary, Sue and her five siblings sent them on a Caribbean cruise. They wrapped the tickets in a box, using a map of the Caribbean as wrapping paper, and presented the gift as if it were an ordinary present at a family dinner.

78. A decorative, personalized family plaque. Include the family name, the year the parents were married and the birthdates of each of the children.

Wedding anniversary

 Create a "family gallery." Put photos of all generations in coordinating frames. Include baby pictures, graduations, weddings, etc.

Ruth and her parents went through a collection of photos together, so Mom and Dad could choose the photos they wanted on the wall. Ruth had enlargements made, purchased matching frames and she and her husband put up all the pictures.

 A photo album or collage filled with pictures of friends and family from past to present.

81. The history of the family name and family crest on parchment can be bought in many malls throughout the country.

 A framed sheet of their wedding song.

83. Have your parents' wedding announcement framed.

84. For your grandparents' anniversary, refurbish an old photo of the couple as newlyweds and put it in a beautiful frame.

 A homemade video. It can commemorate the special couple, review family highlights, include interviews with family and friends or even feature reenactments of memorable events. This makes a great group effort among siblings.

When Mark and Beverly's six children were between the ages of 2 and 12, they wrote, produced and directed a movie starring themselves. Despite bad acting, defective props and no sound, the movie was a big hit. Twenty-five years later the children, along with a few grandchildren, reenacted the original version on videotape. The group enjoys viewing both the original and the remake every time there's a family gathering.

86. Professional window washing. Most people are not fond of the idea of hanging out of a second-story window with a squeegee, no matter what their age.

 A compact disc player and CDs of old favorites. Keep your parents up-to-date with technology, but don't try to change their style. Don't forget to include their wedding song!

88. Video classics. Anything from *Casablanca* to *Attack of the Killer Tomatoes*. Include a big can of popcorn or their favorite snack, and you've just given them a relaxing, nostalgic evening at home.

 Gifts from the garden. Made with tender loving care and inexpensive to give.
AnnMarie grows flowers and herbs, dries them, wraps them in lace and gives them to her mother as potpourri for all occasions.

90. A subscription to a magazine they'd enjoy. Consider *National Geographic, Smithsonian* or a gracious-living magazine.

91. A fruit basket or a subscription to a fruit of the month club. You can send the old favorites or exotic new fruits. One company to try: Harry & David (see Appendix 1 for more information).

92. An answering machine. Some parents are reluctant to adapt to all this "high-tech stuff." They may even feel uncomfortable programming a personal message. Pick out an easy-to-use machine, give them a lesson on basic technology and offer to record a message for them.

 If you're in school, make something for your parents in art class. *When she was in seventh grade, Monika made her parents an "oven rack remover" in shop class. It was a long wooden stick with a groove in the bottom to pull the oven rack out and a V-shape in the front to push the rack back in. Her Mom and Dad appreciate her handiwork every time they use this handy gadget—even though Monika is now 25!*

Father's Day

These gift ideas will work for Dad's birthday, too. Needless to say, if your father has a hobby—fishing, bowling, golf, etc.—his avocation will provide plenty of fodder for ideas. You can get him a fishing T-shirt, a fishing bucket, a tackle box, a fishing rod, a fishing hat... (Check out Chapter 8 for specifics on other hobby-related gifts.) But beyond that, here are some ideas:

94. A hammock. Perfect for lazy days in the shade.

95. A box of cigars (provided he smokes them) and a subscription to the fancy *Cigar Aficionado* magazine.

96. A shaving mirror that hangs in the shower.

97. An engraved pocket watch.

98. For your favorite channel surfer, a subscription to *TV Guide*. A gift like this is good to give around Christmas and Chanukah, because it's easier to keep track of subscriptions when they're started at the beginning of the year.

99. A pair of genuine sheepskin moccasins with shearling lining.

100. A pants press.

 A travel case filled with shaving cream, razors, deodorant, cologne, toothpaste, toothbrush, shampoo and conditioner.

102. A gift certificate to a home improvement store.

103. Sign Dad up with a beer of the month club. Through Beer Across America, Dad will get two six-packs from two different microbreweries and a newsletter each month for approximately $24 a month. Call 800-854-2337.

Father's Day

104. A weather protectant cover for his pride and joy—his car.

105. A bucket filled with car care needs. Auto supply stores carry car care kits, which include sponges, waxes, a variety of cleaning fluids, etc. Traditional dads will appreciate acknowledgment of their role as car caretaker.
Chris bought one of these for his dad at a discount department store. Buying all the materials in one package kept the price down, and his dad loved it—he used it up in no time. Chris already knows what to buy him for the next holiday.

106. Electric shoeshine kit. Dads love to have immaculate shoes.

107. A Swiss army knife. Trust us, he'll use it—whether to cut open the next gift box he receives from you, file his nails or pop open a bottle of wine. Most dads love gadgets—and this is the granddaddy of all gadgets.

108. A monogrammed bowling towel and bowling bag to hold his shoes and ball.

109. A tie, of course. Pick something fun to liven up his wardrobe. A Jerry Garcia original, a Mickey Mouse motif. Whatever his vocation, hobby, favorite cartoon character or even favorite TV sitcom, there's a tie that pays homage. Be creative.

 Boxer shorts. You can find a one-of-a-kind pair featuring glow-in-the-dark aliens in the Johnson Smith catalog (featured in Appendix 1). For the dad who has everything!

111. A decorative pillow for the couch, with a pouch for holding the TV remote control and television guide.

Father's Day

 Designer sunglasses such as Ray-Ban, Oakley, etc.

113. A pair of baseball tickets for you and Dad. Try to get tickets for one of the fan appreciation days, when they give out souvenirs with the team's logo on them.

114. A fishing pole, a trout vest, bait (not live!) and a fishing calendar that shows when the fish are biting.

115. Heavy-duty shelving for the basement or garage, wherever Dad keeps his maintenance materials. Assemble them yourself or have them installed by a professional.

116. The trusty leather wallet, key case or belt. These traditional masculine necessities can always use replacement.

 Wash your parents' car(s). You can commit to doing this just once, for a set period or every week.

118. A portable dishwasher for those who have moved out of a large home and into an apartment without a dishwasher.

119. A contract with a gourmet food delivery service such as Wolferman's (see Appendix 1 for contact information) to have muffins, flavored loaves of bread or another gourmet baked item shipped to Mom and Dad's house each month—for several months or up to a year.

120. An electric blanket—great for those cold winter nights. Get one large enough for your parents to share.

121. Matching thermal underwear.

 A video camera with blank tapes. Make sure you include batteries so it can be used right away.

Mother's Day

Mother's Day and birthdays are perfect times to show our gratitude through gifts. For traditional and radical moms alike, some gifts are all-time pleasers. You'll find these, as well as some more unusual gifts, in this list:

123. An herb garden. You can buy them prepackaged with a variety of herb seeds and pretty pots. Mom can plant the herbs herself and watch them bloom again and again.

 A fancy address book already filled in. Check museum gift shops for artistic prints. Get a hold of Mom's stray phone numbers, business cards, her original, sloppily-kept address book and anything else you think might contain a contact. Enter this information into the new book, neatly and alphabetically. At least for a little while, she won't have any more trouble finding phone numbers!
Regina did this for her mother, whose original book was so disorganized she needed to ask for Regina's college address (which didn't change all four years) at least once a month.

125. A favorite perfume. Buy Mom the powder, body lotion or bath oil to go with it.

126. An elegant crocheted or lace tablecloth.

127. An invitation to high tea. Many upscale hotels serve a full tea in the afternoon, complete with fine china, scones and harp music.

128. Anything from an antique or thrift store. These stores sell some of the most unique items—pillbox hats, blown glass sugar bowls or vases, costume jewelry, wool coats with velvet or fur collars, Gucci bags and more.

129. A basket filled with bath beads, moisturizers, loofah sponges and soaps. She deserves to pamper herself once in a while.

Mother's Day

130. Flowers, of course.

131. A perfume sampler set.

132. Membership to Bath of the Month Club ($29.95). Members receive a startup kit when joining and spa treatments delivered each month thereafter for $9. Call 800-406-2284.

133. A line of genuine salon hair care products. Include shampoo for her specific hair type, clarifying shampoo, daily conditioner and deep conditioner, hot oil treatment, spritz, hair spray, curl booster, gel, mousse, etc.

134. A bread maker for the mom who loves fresh bread but not all the work involved. The house will sure smell good!

 A guardian angel pin. She's been your guardian angel—now give one back to her.

136. A mother's ring with each child's birthstone.

137. A tennis bracelet with each child's birthstone.

138. A basket filled with gourmet spices and cookbooks for the mom who loves to experiment in the kitchen.

 A decorative music box or figurine that plays Mom's favorite tune.

140. A bird whistle, birdseed, bird-identifying guide, etc., creatively arranged in a bird bath.

141. A "sounds of nature" cassette tape or compact disc—sounds of the rainforest, a thundering rainstorm, a babbling brook, the ocean, etc.

142. Wind chimes.
     When Phil spent a night at his friend's parents' home while traveling, he gave them wind chimes to thank them for their hospitality. Although he had never met them before and didn't know their preferences, the wind chimes were much appreciated.

143. A lap desk. Stuffed and fluffy on one side, with a flat board on the other for resting a book, papers, etc. Great for writing letters or reading in bed.

144. A letter opener. A lot safer than using a knife, and available in many styles. Some are even magnetic, so they can be kept on the refrigerator.

145. A gift from your parent's alma mater is always a nice touch.
     Jeanne called the bookstore of the University of Wisconsin, her father's alma mater, and asked for a catalog of their alumni gifts. From the catalog, she ordered an attractive polo shirt with the UW emblem on the pocket. She now considers the catalog a mother lode of gift ideas for her father.

 A handmade card. You can't beat the sentimentality, and your parents will love it—no matter how old you are.

Chapter 3

Kid stuff: Giving great things to small packages

How difficult could it be to buy a kid a gift? Just pick up the latest teen-queen fashion doll or Saturday morning TV's newest mutation of an action toy and you're set, right? After all, you're probably getting lots of help from the gift recipient—we all know just how vocal kids can be about what they want!

But there are pitfalls in present-buying for the precious young. Not the least of which is parental approval. (See how popular *you* are with Mom and Dad after you bring a chemistry set or a 1,000-piece, put-it-together-yourself dollhouse to the party!)

In addition, today's generous benefactor must worry about plenty of other issues: safety issues, gender-identification issues, family values issues and, yes, even energy issues. (It doesn't matter a whit if that super-techtonic laser-controlled robot *can* bake pizza and serve it to the child in bed—if you neglected to include the 25 triple-A batteries required to turn the thing on.)

A few suggestions for selecting a special gift for a child:

- Check with the parents for favorite hobbies or interests. Even a 3-year-old may exhibit an enthusiasm for drawing, playing make-believe games or reading.

- Keep it simple—avoid multipiece gizmos that have to be put together or that require lots of batteries or the purchase of other items before they can be used.

- Follow the age guidelines printed on most toys. (Most packaging includes a message such as "For ages 4 to 6" or "Includes small parts. Not for children under 3.") If in doubt, check with a parent. (Please note that the gifts included in this chapter are in no particular order regarding age-appropriateness.)

- Consider keepsake items—even ones that don't carry as much cachet for the child now. These gifts will remain a treasured memory once a child matures. (How many of us still have one or two really special gifts from childhood—a delicate pearl necklace, a tattered, beloved teddy bear, a weathered first baseball mitt—tucked away in some secret cubbyhole?)

The ideal gift allows the child an opportunity to both play and learn. But don't get pigeonholed into some rigid definition of "education." Just try to remember what it was that made you happy as a child—and take it from there.

147. A child-sized kitchen set, shopping cart, playhouse or toy oven (some really bake!). Kids love to play grown-up.

148. A book/novelty set. For example, a Madeline book packaged with a Madeline doll. Many popular children's storybooks are packaged this way.

149. An ant farm. (Best for older ages. Remind the child to be careful not to drop and break it!)

150. A collection of cartoon videos featuring the child's favorite characters—consider Sesame Street, Loony Tunes, Animaniacs, Disney classics and more.

151. A subscription to a kids' magazine. Possibilities include *Sports Illustrated for Kids*, *Highlights*, *Sesame Street* and others. Consider the child's age and reading level when selecting.

152. A remote-controlled car.

153. A set of walkie-talkies.

For growing minds and budding talent

You can always take the educational route and bestow gifts such as classic books, mind-challenging games or lessons that encourage musical talent. Here are some real parent-pleasers that are also fun for the child who receives them:

154. A world globe. An excellent learning tool for students, as well as a colorful decoration for the bedroom.

155. Software programs for the child who has access to a computer. From games (yay!) to math tutorial programs (yuck).

 A telescope for gazing at the stars—and a book about astronomy.

157. A pair of skates or dance shoes and weekly lessons. This will help teach coordination, especially to the very young.

158. A musical instrument (especially if you're the parent and willing to put up with the noise). It doesn't need to be anything as fancy as a Stradivarius. Just a simple songflute, guitar, clarinet, etc.

159. Weekly lessons to go with the musical instrument.

 Puzzles.

161. A small blackboard, eraser and chalk. Good for children not yet in school, who enjoy pretending they are.

162. A monogrammed towel. You can have a child's towel embellished with a picture—balloons or a sailboat, for example—along with his or her name. Try Lands' End (listed in Appendix 1).

Books

Whether the child is old enough to read or still loves to be read to, you're almost always on the right track by selecting a book as a gift. The challenge is choosing from so many great ones. Here are just a sampling of classics and favorites:

163. *Where the Wild Things Are* by Maurice Sendak.

164. *Green Eggs and Ham, One Fish Two Fish, A Fly Went By, Horton Hatches the Egg*—anything by Dr. Seuss. Every kid loves them, and it's a fun way to get children interested in reading.

165. *The Tale of Peter Rabbit* by Beatrix Potter.

166. *The Giving Tree* by Shel Silverstein, or a book of his poems, such as *A Light in the Attic* and *Where the Sidewalk Ends*. They're classics and fun to read. (Silverstein has some adult-oriented books out there as well, so be sure of the content before you purchase one for a child.)

 For the daring and nonsqueamish, *Everybody Poops* or *The Gas We Pass*—two books published by Kane/Miller Publishers.

168. A collection of nursery rhyme books or fairy tales—all the favorites—*Three Little Pigs, Little Red Riding Hood, The Gingerbread Man*, etc.

169. Storybooks that incorporate the child's name and friends' and pets' names as characters. This is a great way to get kids involved in reading, and it makes them feel special when they see their name in print. Check your local mall for a kiosk that sells these customized storybooks.

170. Goosebump books. These are a hot commodity with preteens these days.

Books

171. Babysitters Club books. These are very popular with teenage and preteen girls.

172. Nancy Drew or Hardy boys mysteries for older readers.

173. A good children's dictionary will promote an interest in learning and be useful in the years to come. (Because they're often illustrated and more entertaining, parents may prefer to use them, too.)

174. A children's encyclopedia. Try the *Fisherking Children's Encyclopedia.*

 Kids' songs on audiocassette or CD. These are great for long drives in the car and are sure to be appreciated by the child's parents.

176. A wooden kid-size rocker in a primary color. Try the L.L. Bean catalog (see Appendix 1 for information).

177. A wooden rocking horse. Along with being fun, this is likely to become a treasured keepsake.

 A face food mold for the kid who's not interested in dinner! Order a mold kit from the Johnson Smith catalog (see Appendix 1) and the child can create a customized gelatin mold in the shape of his or her face.

179. A clock for the child's bedroom. It can have a sports theme, music theme, etc.

180. Hand-held computer games.

 A diary...with lock and key.

Games

Games are a perennial favorite and an excellent way for the whole family to spend fun quality time together, especially on a cold winter day when outdoor activities are limited. Many classics are also available in children's versions.

182. Candyland. Requires no reading. Great for even very young children.

 A kiddie card game assortment with old favorites, including Go Fish!, Crazy Eights, Uno and Old Maid.

184. Chutes and Ladders. This is another one that requires no reading.

185. Dominoes.

186. Monopoly. Also available in a children's version.

187. Checkers.

188. Chess.

189. Parcheesi.

190. Trivial Pursuit. The children's edition.

 A dream catcher. For the child who gets the jitters when the lights go out. According to legend, this Native American feather ornament, if hung above a bed, will ward away nightmares!

192. A Mickey Mouse watch. Truly a classic.

193. A mini piano.

194. A beanbag chair—solid-colored, personalized or decorated with a favorite sports team's logo. This inexpensive classic never goes out of style. A vibrantly colored beanbag chair will quickly become a favorite and is easily transportable from room to room.

195. A collection of child-sized instruments—tambourine, castanets, sleigh bells, rhythm blocks, triangle, jingle stick, xylophone.

 A yo-yo with an instruction book for doing tricky maneuvers.

197. A camping set, including a small tent, canteen, travel containers for products like soap and a toothbrush, and a flashlight.

198. A sleeping bag—great for camping out or sleepovers!

199. A comforter set and sheets with a favorite sports team or cartoon character pictured on them.

 Costume material. Kids adore dressing up, and the more creative the materials to work with, the more fun. Save old makeup for transforming 6-year-olds into stunning princesses or scary monsters. Old nightgowns, slips and lacy blouses become fairy costumes, a housecoat becomes a king's robe and workout gear can be transformed into cat costumes or a ninja getup.

201. An art set in an organized caddie, including crayons, watercolors, markers, paper, etc.

 A stay at a summer camp, whether it's a day camp, sports camp, art institute, sleep-away camp or weight-loss camp. It's a good way to get kids out of their parents' hair for a few weeks and the experience can be a long-treasured childhood memory.

203. A bike.

204. A sandbox.

205. A trampoline.

Gender-specific gifts

Behavioral scientists often say that sexism and the perception of sexual differences can be traced back to childhood—when girls and boys are encouraged to play with different kinds of toys and pursue different forms of playtime. Nevertheless, we feel obligated to offer the following suggestions as gifts that will be preferred by girls and boys respectively.

Girls

206. Birthstone jewelry.

 A pearl necklace. Begin with only one pearl on a chain, then add a graduated pearl for each occasion.

When their six granddaughters were little, Dale and Jerry gave each a necklace with a small, cultured pearl. Every year for Christmas, they've had a jeweler add a half-inch to an inch of graduated pearls. The young ladies will soon have completed pearl necklaces to cherish.

208. A jewelry box, perhaps a musical one.

209. Doll clothes for a favorite doll.

210. A dollhouse assembled, painted and fully furnished. (You can buy a preconstructed dollhouse or do it yourself.) If the child really enjoys it, you can buy accessories for it for years to come.

211. A miniature porcelain teacup set for doll tea parties.

212. A silver or gold nameplate necklace.

213. Barbie and her various friends, family and boyfriend clones.

Gender-specific gifts

 Madame Alexander dolls. These are expensive collectibles, dressed in costumes representing well-known literary characters or international fashion. More for show than playtime, but a lot of fun, particularly for older girls.

215. A charm bracelet. A nice gift and one that will provide opportunities for future gifting as you can continue to add charms for occasions such as First Communion or graduation.

Boys

 Matchbox cars.

217. A train set.

218. A child-sized pinball game, Ping-Pong table or pool table.

 For the little handy-Andy: Make a kid-sized wooden workbench and give tools such as a small saw, hammer, screwdriver, vise, etc.

Joe's grandfather (a carpenter) made a wooden workbench for him when he was 7. Joe boosted it up on cinder blocks and is still using the bench at 27 years old.

220. A baseball cap with a favorite cartoon character or sports team logo depicted on it.

221. A silver or gold identification bracelet.

 A set of nontoxic watercolor paints and a paint-by-numbers book.

223. Winter mittens, gloves, scarves and hats. Kids are always losing them—one can never have too many.

A special event

Plan an afternoon at a favorite place or go to a special kid's event. Please keep in mind, however, that depending on the kid's age, a gift may not be time spent, but a *thing*. So no matter how much quality time you spend together, commemorate it with a quantifiable memento—even if it's just a T-shirt, a cap or a poster. Consider these excursions:

224. An ice-skating extravaganza.

225. A trip to a children's museum, aquarium or planetarium.

226. A movie, complete with popcorn and candy.

227. A day at an amusement park.

228. A game of miniature golf.

 A trip to the local video arcade with an allotment of quarters.

230. A day at an indoor sports amusement park.

231. A day at the circus.

232. A trip to the zoo.

 A day playing paintball with friends. This is a game of team tag played outside—except getting "tagged" means being hit with a burst of paint. Look under "Amusement places" in your local yellow pages for paintball locations. (Not for the very young, since paintball involves the use of paint-splattering guns.)

234. A movie at a drive-in theater. (Let the kids go in their pajamas.)

A special event

235. An overnight camping trip...in your own backyard, with a new tent! (Be sure to include a flashlight—and a key to the back door for those frequent "I'm thirsty" or "I need to use the bathroom" emergencies.)

 A day at a petting zoo. (Just don't play "Pin the Tail on the Donkey"!)

237. A trip to a sporting event. A real treat at any age.

238. Horseback riding.

 A slumber party with a few best friends.

240. Russian nesting dolls. You know, you open up the big doll and inside there's a littler doll, and inside that, a littler doll...

241. Cabbage Patch Kids.

242. Raggedy Ann and Andy.

243. The traditional big stuffed bear.

244. A hammock for stuffed animals.

245. An identification collar for a favorite stuffed animal. It's a cute idea for children who take their favorite stuffed animals everywhere they go—and who would be heartbroken if they lost one.

246. Cassette singles of birthday songs with the child's name in them. These usually can be found in gift and party stores. Playing the personalized tune can become a birthday ritual.

247. A seesaw.

248. A pair of skates (roller-, ice- or in-line) or a skateboard.

 A swingset or outdoor gym.

250. Build a simple treehouse.

251. Legos. Available in many age-appropriate sizes and sets, they're fun and a good "thinking" toy.

252. A colorful detailed kite with lots of streamers—shaped like anything but a kite. Getting one into the air promotes a whimsical sense of accomplishment.

253. A bicycle radio. It connects to the handlebars and is a much safer alternative to riding a bike while listening to music through headphones.

254. A basketball hoop. Some can be installed permanently in a driveway, some are temporary setups that can be put away in the garage or transported to a friend's house. While you're at it, throw in a quality basketball, too.

255. A Sprinkler Pal, Slip 'n' Slide or other water game. Attach to a garden hose, and you're set!

256. A wading pool.

257. A water gun.

258. Water toys for the pool, such as volleyball nets, rafts, beach balls, etc.

 A playhouse.

To encourage saving money

260. A bank folder.
John's parents gave him a "Pocket Pig" bank folder when he was a child. It was filled with 30 brand-new dimes. He still has the Pocket Pig, but he wishes he still had the original dimes. Sentimentally, they'd be worth much more than $3 to him now!

261. Corporate stocks. A wonderful way to teach children about business and finance.

262. A piggy bank—not necessarily a pig, though.

263. A money-wrapping coin bank.

264. A wallet.

 A change purse.

266. A kids' business book, like *Fast Cash for Kids* by Bonnie and Noel Drew. Great for encouraging kids to become young entrepreneurs.

267. Nerf-type toys. Parents will certainly appreciate these spongy toys—a Nerf basketball can be tossed around indoors without breaking anything!

268. A small pet, such as a guinea pig, gerbil, hamster—but only if you're the parent and you know your child truly wants to take the responsibility of caring for another living thing, and *you* are willing to take the responsibility of cleaning the cage, purchasing the food, etc.

269. A battery-operated, walking, barking puppy or meowing cat. (For the·child who's not yet ready to assume the responsibility of a *live* pet.)

270. Beach toys—a big colorful ball, shovel and pail, sand sifters and more.

271. Swimming lessons.

272. A big, cartoon-inspired beach towel for vacations or summer camp.

273. A child-sized sports car, dump truck, tractor or other car that looks like a mini version of the real thing and that the child can "drive" around the neighborhood! (A step above the Big Wheel.) Some are motorized, some are pedal-powered.

274. A helmet for bike riding. A bike helmet is a requirement for children in some states...and a good idea in any state.

 A Wiffle ball and bat.

276. A snow sled.

277. A full set of everything required for playing the child's favorite sport. For example, for a child interested in soccer, provide cleats, a soccer ball, kneepads, a net—and goalie gear, if desired.

278. A good kids' cookbook along with a kid-size apron. So it can be put to use immediately, provide the ingredients for one of the recipes.

279. A View-Master—a plastic mini-projector held in front of the eyes to view, in 3-D format, still-life scenes on a disk that advances to the next scene when you press a lever. Disks feature scenes from children's movies like *Cinderella* or *Pinnocchio*, as well as other subjects of interest to kids, such as dinosaurs or spaceships. Buy a few disk sets to go along with it.

School days

No matter how anxious kids are to get out of school at the beginning of summer, they're almost always eager to return in the fall. And new supplies, books, gadgets and other school-related accessories always add to the excitement. Whether launching the scholastic career for your favorite first-grader or celebrating a fall birthday for an elementary-age niece or nephew, here are some sure-to-please ideas:

280. A lunchbox or colorful insulated lunch bag.

 A set of printed encyclopedias for reference. Although interactive encyclopedias on CD-ROM are highly recommended, there's still nothing like having *real* books in your hands.

282. A backpack.

 A "school memories" book for recording achievements and other facts and holding photos from each year of school, from first grade to eighth grade.

284. A calculator.

285. School supplies: a stapler, staples and staple remover, roll tape, paper clips, rubber bands, Post-it Notes, a ruler, pens (erasable ones are helpful for the neatness-challenged!), pencils (send away for decorated, personalized ones), a highlighter, correction fluid, an eraser, a notepad, book covers, glue, etc. Use your imagination to create a gift basket—put them all in a brand-new knapsack, storage bin or wastebasket.

School days

286. A desk.

287. A bookcase.

288. A personalized book embosser encourages children to build a personal library of books.

289. A puppet. There are some very elaborate ones, but if you're feeling creative, you can knit or make one. Patterns are available at craft stores, and you can use anything from buttons for eyes to a sock for the body of the puppet.

 A novelty bed, such as one shaped like a race car. These beds could make a kid actually look forward to bedtime.

291. A cedar chest. Adds a decorative touch and can hold important keepsakes from childhood into adulthood. If it's well cared for, it will last a lifetime.

 A bead kit for making necklaces and bracelets. Good for older kids—both boys and girls. From a craft store, purchase an ample amount of elastic string and beads in different colors and sizes. Assemble beads by color and size in a plastic craft storage box with compartments. Handpaint the child's name on the top of the lid, if you like.

 Coloring books with a new box of crayons.

294. A plastic dinnerware set with a favorite cartoon character or action figure pictured on the utensils, cups, plates and bowls.

295. A tape recorder or radio/cassette player. The great thing about this gift? You'll know what to get next time—cassettes of stories or songs!

First Communion

First Communion is a Roman Catholic sacrament, celebrated by children ages 7 to 9. It commemorates the first time they receive the Eucharist. Children attend months of special classes to prepare for this event. This is a time when they begin to discover the basic tenets of their faith. They often receive money and other kinds of gifts, but the most appropriate gifts are traditional religious items, such as:

296. A gold or silver crucifix necklace.

297. A set of crystal rosary beads.

298. A framed religious picture.

    Eileen's grandparents gave her a picture of the Last Supper. It was an appropriate gift then, but what makes it special to her now, more than 30 years later, is that they addressed it to her on the back, with the date and the occasion.

299. A Bible embossed with the child's name or initials.

300. An illustrated children's Bible.

 A Bible that has been handed down from generation to generation.

    Claire received a Bible, in a glossy-finished, wooden case, that had once belonged to her great-aunt. The original inscription from her great-aunt's mother was on the cover page.

302. An Etch-a-Sketch.

 Car games for a child who is preparing for a vacation or trip.

For newborns and toddlers

Included in this section are the colorful, whimsical, dazzling toys that babies and toddlers will coo and giggle over. For more baby gift suggestions, see Chapter 6, which covers the topic from the parents' perspective.

304. A mobile of tiny stuffed animals and enclosed bells to hang over a crib or playpen.

305. A set of wooden blocks with letters and numbers on their faces.

306. A classical music recording that is based on a story, such as *Peter and the Wolf* or *Night on Bald Mountain*. Often such recordings are accompanied by a book the child can read when older, but the music can be played to soothe the baby to sleep.

 A set of arm floats for swimming.

308. Stuffed animals, of course.

309. A hardbound, glossy-paged, gilt-edged book of Mother Goose nursery rhymes or a collection of classic fairy tales.

310. Soft, touchy books.

 Squeaky rubber bath toys and colorful bath sponges.

312. A plastic faucet shield to protect the child's head from the tub faucet. These come in various shapes, such as an elephant with the water squirting from its trunk or a whale with the water spouting from its blowhole.

313. A colorful rain ensemble with a matching rain hat, coat, galoshes and umbrella—especially if it's a transparent vinyl umbrella decorated with pictures or cartoons.

 A personalized storybook you wrote, illustrated and bound yourself. If you have a color printer and an illustration or graphics program, you can whip one up right on a computer!

315. A favorite Disney or animated video.

316. A shower radio—fun for bath-lovers and -haters alike.

317. An electric toothbrush in a cartoon-character shape.

 A tape recording of yourself reading a bedtime story. A great idea if you're the grandparent. You can make a new tape each year until there's a collection that the child, as an adult, can play for his or her own children. Your voice will become a legacy.

 Cable TV, or if the family already has cable, upgrade the package so it includes the Disney channel.

320. A simple point-and-shoot camera. A few big-name toymakers make colorful ones just for children.

321. A duffel bag for overnight trips. As useful for a trip to Grandma's as for a scout camping expedition.

322. A piñata. Originating from Mexico and Central America, this papier-mâché figure is decorated with colorful streamers and filled with candy, toys and party favors. It hangs from the ceiling while blindfolded partygoers take turns whacking it with a stick until it breaks open, sending the contents to the ground. Children usually dive for the goodies with great excitement. A good gift to bring to a child's birthday party, it can be purchased at party supply stores.

Party favors, stocking stuffers, etc.

Here are some goodies (traditional and trendy favorites alike) to fill up stockings, to give just for fun, to supplement a larger gift or to reward good behavior at the doctor's office, a no-cavity report from the dentist, a lost tooth, a good grade...

323. Jacks.

324. Bubbles.

325. Colored chalk for playing hopscotch.

326. A jump rope.

327. A pinwheel.

328. A plastic snow globe.

329. Pogs and slammers. A hot trend right now, these are milkcap-sized cardboard disks used in tossing games.

330. A Slinky.

331. Soap crayons. They look like crayons and clean like soap. Children can have a blast writing on bath tiles and all over themselves—and still end up clean in the process.

332. Marbles.

333. A Pez dispenser with candy refills.

334. A boomerang.

 A star. The International Star Registry will name a star for the child and mail a certificate. Call 800-282-3333.

336. A donation to a children's-related charity, such as UNICEF.

337. Plant a tree in the child's name. There are a lot of programs through which you can do this; Jewish organizations sometimes sponsor plant-a-tree-in-Israel programs and many national parks offer plant-a-tree programs, as well.

 Adopt a whale in the child's name. The International Wildlife Coalition (IWC) sponsors the Whale Adoption Project. You make a donation and pick a specific whale that IWC has been tracking in the wild. The child will receive a description of the whale, stickers, newsletters and discounts for whale-watching tours. Contact IWC at 508-548-8328.

Chapter 4

Hot gifts
for cool teens

There's no getting out of it. Even if you were farsighted enough to remain childless when you realized that having babies would lead to having teenagers, there will come a time, inevitably, when you will have to buy a teenager a gift. Yes, your sister's child will one day celebrate that 13th birthday, you'll be invited to the bar mitzvah of a co-worker's son, your best friend's daughter will celebrate her "Sweet 16" or your baby sitter will graduate from high school.

For the gift-giving challenged, buying gifts for teenagers can be one of the *most* challenging tasks of all. While teens appreciate gifts as much as any gift recipient (and they certainly seem to be in a constant state of *need*—"I need new shoes," "I need that CD," "I need a new car"), they're very, very particular. Yes, they do love music. But what *kind* of music? Which *artist* do they prefer? And what recordings do they already have? And they *do* love clothes. But which brand? What style?

For the uninitiated, buying a gift that will make a teenager happy may seem like an impossible mission. However, there are solutions. *Plenty* of them. And you'll discover 130 in this chapter. But don't pass up Chapter 8 if you're gift-hunting for a teen with a hobby or special interest.

339. Money. While it may not be incredibly creative, money is universally appreciated by teens. Giving money takes all the risk out of buying something that will elicit smirks or groans, will be buried in a closet—or returned.

340. A savings bond. You can buy a $50 bond for just $25.

Gift certificates

You want to give something more "personal" than money, but you don't want to make a *faux pas* regarding teen tastes? A gift certificate is a great—and safe—way to go! Consider these ideas:

341. A gift certificate from a clothing store. Opt for casual clothing and names that have some cachet for teens. Safe bets might be The Gap, Urban Outfitters, Banana Republic—or even a major department store that carries a good selection of casual clothes.

342. A gift certificate from a music store. Selecting music for teenagers whose preferences you don't know could end in disaster. Better leave the decision-making to them.

343. A gift certificate from a video store, to be used for purchases or rentals of movies or video games.

344. A gift certificate from a store that sells athletic shoes. We don't get it, but the teenagers we know seem to be obsessed with such footwear. Boys *and* girls. And, evidently, you can never have too many pairs. This from the mother of a 16-year-old who has threatened to report her for child abuse because she only buys him athletic shoes every three months.

345. A gift certificate for a pair of designer sunglasses.

 A gift certificate from a favorite fast-food place. For a relatively small investment, you can keep a hungry youth in hamburgers, burritos or pizza for a month.

Big-ticket items ($100 and *way* up)

So there's this one special teenager you really like or you're related to in a big way (like you're his mom or a rich uncle or something). What are some big-splurge gift ideas that are sure to please?

347. Membership to a fitness center. Depending upon the program, you can sign up the teenager for a few months or a year or more. Costs vary, but monthly payments are generally less than $50.

348. A computer. A major investment, so make sure it meets the teen's needs. Find out whether he or she uses a Mac or PC in school, for example.

349. A futon, full-size, and frame. It folds into an attractive couch by day, saving space and giving the teen's room a more sophisticated appearance.

350. A video camera. For the budding director—or the budding ham.

351. Luggage: Get a whole set or just a couple of good, sturdy pieces.

352. A stereo system or a portable CD player.

353. A mutual fund. Some can be started for as little as $500.

354. A bicycle (a good idea for the college-bound graduate).

355. A car (like we said, big-ticket items).

356. A round-trip plane ticket to visit a friend or relative in a faraway place (a particularly popular idea if it's spring break time and the location is someplace warm and exotic).

357. A telephone. All kinds are out there—from standard touch-tones to novelty shapes such as sports cars, fish and other animals, Coke cans, old-time radios, cartoon characters and more.

358. A camera. Unless he or she is an avid photographer (which probably means he/she already owns a more sophisticated model than you could afford), one of those auto-everything cameras that require minimal fiddling is probably the best bet.

359. A really good calculator. Math students and future engineers will appreciate a more advanced model.

360. A portable cassette/radio.

361. A CD rack or storage receptacle.

362. A CD or cassette carrying case.

363. A carry-on or tote. If you know the teen has other luggage, see if you can find a matching piece or one that complements the set.

364. A magazine subscription. Think of the individual's interests. Consider *Rolling Stone, Sports Illustrated, Seventeen, Thrasher*.

365. Membership to a favorite organization, such as Greenpeace, PETA or even the fan club of a favorite recording star or celebrity. Membership often includes a magazine or newsletter subscription, which will keep the teen hooked into the activities and developments of his or her pet cause.

366. Speaking of philanthropic causes, another great idea for the community-minded is to give a donation in the name of the teenager.

 T-shirts and baseball caps. Virtually safe gifts for either sex. Regarding T-shirts, you don't have to worry about being too exact in size (when in doubt, go large). When choosing, think in terms of favorite schools or sports teams. Avoid "cute" messages—this may not be the image the teenager wishes to convey.

For the new driver

368. A really cool key chain.

369. Membership to a road service.

370. A personalized license plate—that is, if a more *affluent* relative or friend bought the teen his or her own car.

371. Several vouchers for deluxe car washes.

 Car knickknacks

372. A hanging garbage bag and air fresheners.

373. A change holder.

374. A sun visor.

375. A traveling cup.

For car emergencies

376. A pack-in-the-trunk emergency kit, complete with flares, jumper cables, a visor for front window with a "Help! Call Police" message on one side, a flashlight, a thermal blanket and a gas can.

377. A good backpack—sturdy enough to hold a lockerful of heavy notebooks and schoolbooks.

378. A leather wallet or billfold.

379. A bulletin board.

Books

Whether they want to or not, teenagers will undoubtedly find themselves in a situation where they have to read. Classics from Shakespeare to Salinger will be on the school's required reading list for many. A thoughtful gift for young teenagers, whatever the occasion, might be a collection of classics or an attractive hardbound edition of one. Based on current reading lists from high schools around the country, here are some ideas.

380. *A Tale of Two Cities* by Charles Dickens.

381. *The Great Gatsby* by F. Scott Fitzgerald.

382. *The Odyssey* by Homer.

383. *Treasure Island* by Robert Louis Stevenson.

384. *Canterbury Tales* by Chaucer.

385. A set of Shakespearean plays.

386. *Moby Dick* by Herman Melville. Although this is one case where the authors unanimously agree that it's worth the risk of English-teacher wrath to go straight for the Cliff Notes.

 Speaking of Cliff Notes, the authors recommend a pictorial alternative—*Classic Comics* offers noteworthy literature ranging from *Faust* to *Uncle Tom's Cabin* in comic book form.

388. Or how about a movie version of a required reading classic? Whether it's Ernest Hemingway's *A Farewell to Arms* or Tennessee Williams's *The Glass Menagerie*, there's probably a classic video that could add new insight—as well as entertainment value. (Note: Lest we attract an angry boycott by English teachers across the country, we don't mean to imply that these ideas should be substitutes for actually *reading* the text, but merely used as an additional tool for greater understanding!)

Experiences

389. A day of horseback riding.

 For the adventurous: a flight lesson with a local small craft airport.

391. A day with a friend at a nearby theme park (no parents).

392. Dinner with a friend at the nearest Hard Rock Cafe or Planet Hollywood.

393. Tickets to a music concert.

394. Tickets to a sports event.

395. Sessions with a personal trainer. (Most teens, boys *and* girls, are eager to learn the *right* way to work out, lift weights, get in shape or build muscle. A single session may cost as little as $20.)

396. Lessons. To play it safe, you really do need to know the teen's interests. Once that's determined, your imagination's the limit. Consider tennis, ice-skating, dancing, scuba diving, rock-climbing, etc.

 A videotape of friends, with music and effects (make copies and give them as graduation presents to the whole group).

398. A basketball net—one that hangs over the garage or one of those portable jobs.

399. A pair of in-line skates—include safety pads and helmet.

400. A sleeping bag.

Confirmation

The Catholic church, as well as some other Christian denominations, has a confirmation ceremony for teenagers who've completed their religious education, typically at the age of 14 or 15. Teenagers going through confirmation will, of course, appreciate "generic" gifts, but religion-oriented gifts are an important consideration. Here are a few suggestions:

401. Jewelry of religious significance, such as a crucifix or favorite saint's medal.

402. A prayer book with the teen's name embossed on the cover.

403. Rosary beads.

404. A cross or special prayer framed for hanging.

405. A Boogie board (a small surfboard) for the beach.

 Scented candles or incense and a ceramic incense holder.

407. Aromatherapy oils: Different scents have different "powers." Some energize, others relax. They're fun, relatively inexpensive and can be found in specialty shops such as The Body Shop (see Appendix 1) and Bath and Body Works.

 Earrings. Check for holes in the ears (possibly even nose, tongue or navel). If you're not sure about styles, check with the clerk. Typically, it's safer to buy two or three inexpensive pairs instead of one more pricey name-brand pair.

409. A monogrammed garment bag.

 Healing crystals in necklace form. Some are said to make the wearer smarter, more attractive, stronger, etc.

Bar/bat mitzvahs

At the age of 13, Jewish boys and girls celebrate bar mitzvahs and bat mitzvahs respectively. These are the "coming-of-age" ceremonies in which the celebrant assumes adult religious responsibilities, such as chanting from the Bible and perhaps leading a Sabbath service. A party often follows the service, and while money is a popular gift—as well as the types of things you might give for graduation (dictionaries, pen and pencil sets)— items of religious significance should also be considered. If you don't know the child, or are unfamiliar with Jewish religious customs, check at the synagogue gift shop where the bar mitzvah will be held, and the salespeople there will be a great help. Often, it's customary for the child to "register" at the gift shop, so you'll know exactly what he or she needs or wants.

411. A menorah for celebrating Chanukah.

412. Candlesticks for the Sabbath.

413. A "tzedakah" box for collecting change for charity.

414. A Kiddush cup—a ritual wine cup.

415. Necklaces, bracelets or rings of religious significance featuring a star of David, the "chai" sign for life or a mezuzah.

416. For the sports lover, a ball of his or her choice, be it a basketball, football, soccer ball, tennis balls—even a beach ball.

417. Software programs. From games to tutorials, these vary in price and *can* cost hundreds, but there are many that cost $50 or less.

 Computer disk organizers.

Sweet 16

A tradition in certain parts of the country, the Sweet 16 party is given for girls. Similar to a big birthday bash or a bat mitzvah, it usually means dress-up, dancing, DJs—and gifts, of course. The following ideas can also be considered for teenage girls in general—whether for birthday, bat mitzvah or graduation.

 A special heirloom (a great aunt's ring, for example).

420. A friendship ring (as long as you're actually a friend).

421. A jewelry box.

422. A silver hairbrush, comb and mirror set.

423. Tickets to a musical.

424. A matching photo album and picture frame.

425. A roomy, attractive cosmetic case with plastic holders for soap, shampoo and lotion.

 Makeup samples. Anyone who's ever bought a major department store mascara has probably picked up a "free gift" containing items that she never uses—lipsticks the wrong color, fragrances the wrong scent or facial products for the wrong skin type. Don't throw them out or let them languish in a cosmetic case in your bathroom closet. Collect a handful of lipsticks, scents, lotions and other cosmetics and buy a pretty box, basket or dish to wrap them in.

427. Appliances such as hairdryers, travel-size irons, curling irons, etc.

428. A photo session at one of those "glamour" portrait studios.

429. A mouse pad with personality—such as one depicting Edward Munch's "The Scream," for example.

430. A put-it-together-yourself computer desk. These can be found for less than $100.

Graduation

College-bound or leaving home

431. A good tool kit.

432. A bed cover: a pretty quilt, a cozy down comforter or a throw in school colors.

433. A radio-alarm clock.

434. A bean bag chair, plain or with a favorite sports team's logo.

435. A husband—not the *marrying* kind, but the *cushion* kind you lean against while studying in bed.

436. For the college-dorm-bound, a good bathrobe for hiking down the halls to the floor bathroom.

437. Organizers! Space is limited in most dorm rooms—even shared apartments—so closet, drawer and desk organizers will be valued. They come in a variety of styles and price ranges, from cardboard, under-the-bed boxes to wicker sliding baskets.

438. A fancy address book.

 A box of assorted greeting cards/stationery.

440. Personalized stationery.

441. A calendar for the upcoming year with important dates already marked.

Graduation:
Work and study aids

442. A *big* dictionary—not one of those pocket dictionaries or an edition that's so old, it doesn't include words such as "database." If you want to go big-ticket, consider *Webster's Third New International Dictionary of the English Language,* which can cost more than $100. But you can find a good, fat one, such as *The American Heritage Dictionary,* for as little as $35.

443. A thesaurus. Recommended: the current edition of *Roget's International Thesaurus.*

444. *The Dictionary of Cultural Literacy.* Great for teenagers as a graduation gift. The source to find out where the expression "cutting the Gordion knot" originates from and other interesting minutiae. A veritable compendium of essential trivia for would-be *literati.*

445. Other desk reference books. Consider *The Encyclopedia of World Geography* for history majors, *The Chicago Manual of Style* or *Bartlett's Quotations* for writers.

 A resume. Every job hunter needs one. If you've got the expertise—and access to a computer—offer to do it yourself. Or present a certificate to be used at a professional resume service.

447. A classy pen and pencil set.

448. Day planner/organizer system. There are a lot on the market, ranging in complexity and price. Choose one that allows flexibility.

 A leather briefcase, monogrammed. (If the teen is going into art or design, consider a portfolio.)

Work and study aids

450. A study pillow. This is sort of a portable desk. Cushioned on one side and a desktop on the other, it's useful for doing homework while sitting in bed.

451. A desk reading light—great for studying without disturbing the roommate.

452. A mini-recorder with microcassettes for ideas or lectures.

453. For a business major: "business cards" (lots of opportunity here to be creative).

454. For a business major: a subscription to *The Wall Street Journal*.

455. For a premed student: a leather medical bag.

456. For a psychology major: a subscription to *Psychology Today*.

457. For an engineering major: a subscription to *Mechanical Engineering*.

458. For an English major: a current copy of *Writer's Market*.

459. A high-quality, expensive bookmark—a pewter clip with a gemstone, for example.

460. Decorative bookends—not the ordinary, metal, stationery-store variety. Think stone elephants or brass dollar signs, or something related to the student's field of study.

461. A really good sheet set (300-thread count).

 A write-on, wipe-off message board for the outside of the dorm room door.

463. Ice-cube trays with stars, moons or different shapes.

 A selection of flavored coffees. (We recommend instant— students may not have access to a bean grinder, espresso machine or even a basic coffeemaker in a dorm room or while studying in the library.)

465. A few prepaid calling cards—or one with *a lot* of time on it that doesn't expire right away.

466. For the intrepid overseas exchange student or backpacker, an electrical currency converter with adapter plugs.

467. Toys for the dorm room, such as a dartboard, Hacky Sack, deck of cards, chess or backgammon board. (These provide a great way to attract new friends.)

468. A subscription to a gossipy magazine sent to the dorm or apartment. (*People, US, Entertainment Weekly*, etc.)

469. A stuffed animal dressed in the logo or team uniform of the college he or she plans to attend.

Chapter 5

Truly engaging gifts for your sweetheart

♥ David, not known for his romantic sensibilities, has been "gently" reminded by Kim that the anniversary of their first date is coming up. After the Chia Pet debacle on Valentine's Day, he's understandably nervous. He does care about Kim and wants to make her happy. What is an appropriate gesture of his affection? Flowers? Jewelry? And does this mean he has to forgo Monday night football?

♥ For the past 44 years, Joe and Edie have adhered to their anniversary tradition: Joe gives Edie money for a dress and they go out to dinner. Joe wants to break tradition for their 45th— way past "silver" and not quite "gold." But Edie hates parties and Joe can't afford that Hawaiian cruise they've talked about. What's left?

♥ Leyna is miserable. She and Scott had their first date two weeks ago. His birthday is in five days. She wants to acknowledge it in a special way, but without overdoing it, because he's not quite a "significant other" yet. While she *is* interested she doesn't want to appear too eager—in case the interest is not mutual. On the other hand, she doesn't want to seem aloof. "What a mess," Leyna moans, "Why couldn't it have been *my* birthday first?"

Have you noticed that couples often break up right before Valentine's Day, Christmas and other major gift-giving occasions? We have friends—men and women alike—who swear that it's easier to *end* a relationship than it is to deal with the flak they may get for either not getting a present or getting the wrong present.

Whether you've been dating for a week or have been married for half a century, finding the right gift for that significant other is no insignificant accomplishment. In fact, it's fraught with emotional dangers, as we've seen in the examples that introduce this chapter.

Well, we don't claim to be relationship experts and we certainly can't tell David, Joe or Leyna, with any certainty, what will make their mates happy. But what we *can* do is offer lots of gift *suggestions* to consider for your significant other. They range from the traditional to the titillating, from the romantic to the risqué—with lots of practical, original, inexpensive, fun, funny and surefire pleasers in between.

470. A certificate for a couples' massage class. You may want to present the certificate in a basket along with scented massage oils.

 A body massager. This full-seat cushion has a panel that controls speed, which areas of your back or legs to massage and intensity of vibrations. (Check out specialty shops such as The Sharper Image or Brookstone. Catalog information for both stores is listed in Appendix 1.)

472. Fragrances. Pick your favorite (hopefully it's both of yours) and expand beyond the expected perfume or cologne. Consider bath foam, shower gel, body lotion, powder.

 A homemade coupon book with coupons good for personal services from you, such as a back rub, breakfast in bed, getting out of an argument, etc.

474. A watch. A great gift solution, whether for a momentous occasion or as a middle-of-the-relationship-road gift. It can say "special," but not necessarily "committed," depending on the price, which can range from inexpensive to very pricey.

475. A brewing kit for the man or woman who enjoys beer. Order for about $59 from Wine Hobby, 800-847-HOPS. You can also find brewing kits at some liquor stores.

 A lava lamp. It's a funky and romantic way to light a room.

Valentine's Day

This holiday may present the biggest challenge to "involved" individuals who consider themselves gift-giving dysfunctional. Most people take the easy way out—a card, flowers or a box of candy, which are all perfectly acceptable options. But here are some other ideas, as well as some creative thoughts on gift presentation.

477. You wearing a bow on your head—and a lacy red teddy or boxers patterned with hearts and flowers.

478. A dozen red roses, although traditional, always has a heart-pounding affect on the recipient. However, you might want to be a little more creative. How about choosing a flower that your loved one really loves—whether simple daisies or exotic orchids? Or select a number that has special meaning for the two of you: seven sunflowers because you've been together seven years, 15 carnations because you met on the 15th, etc.

479. A "bouquet" of red, heart-shaped balloons delivered to your valentine's workplace—or awaiting him or her at home.

 Adult chocolates—X-rated! We're not giving any examples here...you're on your own!

481. Breakfast in bed. If you really want to fancy it up, arrange for a catering service to prepare an elegant breakfast in your kitchen and serve it to you and your valentine.

482. A full-fledged picnic—on the living room floor if a romantic outdoor spot isn't accessible.

Valentine's Day

483. A night at a romantic bed-and-breakfast or an elegant hotel.

484. A candlelit dinner in an off-the-wall place—on the roof of your apartment building, in the park, on the beach. (In most parts of the country, it's pretty nippy around Valentine's Day—so be sure to bring blankets and a thermos of hot cider or Irish coffee!)

485. Serenade your significant other outside his or her window. Find some *good* friends who play instruments to jazz it up a bit.

 Write a love poem. It doesn't have to be a masterpiece, it doesn't even have to rhyme in order to move your loved one with your sentiments.

487. A tape of music you've compiled that has special meaning to the two of you—the song that was playing when you first met, songs whose lyrics convey a message or a feeling, or even goofy stuff.

 Write a song—and sing it.

489. A sexy photo of *you*. Usually available at malls, they require the photo subject to go through somewhat of a makeover. Then he or she is photographed in alluring, model-like poses.

490. Dedicate a song on the radio, on a station you know he or she listens to at a particular time.

491. If you work in the same vicinity as your loved one, sneak into his or her company parking lot at lunchtime and leave a single red rose along with a romantic note on the car.

492. A bonsai tree (if he or she is responsible) and instructions for its care. These trees require love and commitment, as does your relationship.

 Adopt your significant other's favorite zoo animal in his or her name. The zoo will send information about the animal and probably extend special membership privileges.

494. A dual-headed shower system. (Saves water, not necessarily time!)

495. Membership to a wine-of-the-month club. International Wine Cellars is a service that ships two bottles of wine and a newsletter each month, for about $15.95 per month. You can sign up for as little as two months. Call 800-854-2337.

 A book of classic love sonnets.

497. A basic auto repair course. These are offered for a minimal fee at many community schools. It's not the most romantic thing under the sun, but it will give your partner (and you) peace of mind.

498. *Your* frequent flyer miles.

499. A singing telegram, such as an Elvis or a balloon-bearing gorilla to visit him or her at work.

 A ceramic mug with *your* mug and personalized greeting on it.

Joan had a boyfriend who liked a photo of her so much that he photocopied it and put it on his cubicle wall at work. That gave Joan an idea: She had the color original copied onto a ceramic mug with the caption "Kiss me, you cheeky monkey" under the picture. She filled it with Hershey's Hugs and Kisses and gave it to him for Valentine's Day.

For him

How's this for a stereotype? Men want "toys." Big, electronic or motorized items. No teddy bears or dinners by candlelight. Well, it's not true. Okay, it's half-true. Men can be just as sentimental as women even though it doesn't always seem that way. If you can't afford a new motorcycle or a big-screen TV, here are some less expensive suggestions:

501. A tie with a cartoon character design for the guy who's still a child at heart—think Mickey Mouse, Peanuts or Dr. Seuss.

502. Or if he's on the serious side, a silk "power" tie.

 If your significant other is a member of a fraternity, you can consider this a source of gift ideas. Consider a cross-stitch of his fraternity crest, or make him a "badge box" in which to keep his fraternity pin.

Deirdre bought a small, plain wooden box and painted it in Craig's organization's colors and symbols. She decorated it with felt and wooden letters and finished it off with a small cushion inside to put the badge on. Craig was able to keep his badge protected from any other jewelry, yet always knew where to find it.

504. Jewelry. Yes, men do wear jewelry. Consider his preferences and style. A simple gold engraved bracelet if he's conservative; a diamond earring, if he's not.

505. A hat—*not* a baseball cap. Something to fit his fantasies. Maybe a 10-gallon cowboy hat, a felt fedora, a "starving-artist" beret or a pirate hat. Have fun with this.

506. Membership to Boxers of the Month Club. A different and unique pair of designer boxer shorts arrives every month. Call 800-746-7875.

For him

507. A fog-free shower mirror. Many come with suction cups for easy installation and travel purposes.

508. The entire line of his favorite scent (cologne, soap, aftershave, talc, etc.) or as many as you can afford. It's probably something to which he wouldn't typically treat himself.

 A coupon for a day of *no* responsibilities or expectations. Is he responsible for the lawn care? Running the weekend errands? Offer him a day when he doesn't have to do a thing that is usually expected of him. (You may even tell him he can throw his dirty socks on the floor instead of the hamper...but make sure he knows this gift is for only *one* day!)

510. Have one of his favorite posters framed.

511. A huge basket of the toiletries he loyally uses but hates to go out and purchase—deodorant, soap, toothpaste, moisturizer, cotton swabs, tissues, razor refills. Throw in some brands he has never tried but you think he would like.

512. A couch potato kit. Usually made of leather or vinyl, this pouch hangs over the side of a chair or recliner and holds a TV guide and a remote control. Some even have a place to rest a glass.

513. Turn the tables: Send *him* flowers. Send the same amount of flowers as your years together. Spice this up with a romantic or risqué message on the enclosed card.

514. A new leather belt.

515. A fancy new wallet monogrammed with his initials.

For her

Most women claim that anything their sweetheart gets them will be cherished—as long as there is thought and care put into the selection. We would add that what you select says a lot about how you perceive her—or at least how *she* perceives that you perceive her! One of the authors reveals that she knew things were going downhill when her boyfriend brought home a box from a local lingerie store. Instead of the lacy teddy she hoped for, she unwrapped a pair of flannel pajamas emblazoned with a large cartoon cat. Our advice? Unless she specifically asked for those fuzzy houseslippers, stick to the sexy, the racy, the feminine or the frivolous. Consider the practical and the sensible as supplemental.

One of the safest routes to take with a female is jewelry. There's enough range in style and price that you can consider jewelry no matter what the status of your relationship is. A fun watch or a pair of earrings is a great birthday option for the newly dating. And, of course, at the other end of the spectrum is the *engagement ring* for the man who's ready to take the big step. Following are some jewelry suggestions—as well as plenty of other great ideas:

 If the time is right...an engagement ring! Obviously, you don't need this book to give you the idea for a present this important, but here are some things to keep in mind: Many couples today pick out rings together. However, you may want to surprise her with a ring that you picked out yourself. If you are going to take this route, it may be worth it to take her shopping to see what types of settings (and diamonds or other stones) she likes. Then you'll know her tastes, and she'll still be surprised—and pleased—with the ring *and* the proposal.

517. And if you are already married, now's the time to upgrade her ring in some way—perhaps a bigger stone or a new setting.

For her

 A strand of pearls.

519. A crystal pendant. Crystals are said to have certain "powers"—some increasing fertility, offering health or bringing happiness. Select one that's supposed to bring everlasting love.

 A tennis bracelet.

521. A watch bracelet.

522. A necklace with a "love" charm—a heart, a cupid—on it.

 A surprise home-cooked meal with candles, music and, if necessary, the kids away for the night. This is especially appreciated if she is used to cooking for you and the kids on a regular basis.

524. Give her the TV remote control for the entire week. (It's a tough one, but it sure shows that you're in love.)

525. A designer handbag.

526. A certificate to have a "color consultation." Department store makeup counters always offer makeovers and consultations, but some stores also have experts that will assess and match you up with your best colors for clothing.

527. A day at a spa offering a massage, beauty makeover and manicure.

 A shopping spree. Get her a gift certificate to her favorite store. Or better yet, most malls offer gift certificates that can be used at any store in the mall. This way her options are greater.

For her

 Never underestimate the power of a single, red, long-stemmed rose.

530. Mother's Day: We address this holiday at length in Chapter 2, but when children are young, it will be Dad's responsibility to ensure Mom's happiness on this day. A most-appreciated gift might be time alone. Plan to take complete responsibility for the kids this day. Take them to the park, a movie, the zoo, Grandma's...and give Mom some time to herself.

 A homemade collage. Fun to put together and fun to look at. *Steve didn't want to give Dawn a store-bought gift for their third anniversary of dating. He found a sturdy piece of poster board and glued on pictures of them (and friends and family) together, words from magazines relating to all those little "private jokes" they had and even pasted on some matchbooks, postcards and napkins from places they had been together. Needless to say, Dawn was touched and impressed!*

532. Tickets to a show at a comedy club. This is a great idea for a new dating relationship. Even though you may not know the other person well yet, it never hurts to share a laugh.

533. Dancing lessons—ballroom, tango, line dancing, whatever—for the two of you.

534. If your sweetie has expressed an interest in something, but won't follow through for financial or practical reasons, make the dream come true. Buy a pair of ice skates if she admires elegant figure skaters or buy him some canvases and paints if he's always wanted to express himself through art. Show you have faith in his or her desires.

Anniversary

While friends and family members may acknowledge your anniversary with cards, gifts or well-wishes, it's *most* important that *you* remember the occasion in a special way—one that will signify how much you cherish your loved one. How did the ritual of anniversaries start, anyway? We don't know the answer to that question, but we *do* know one thing: Anniversaries are not to be missed. If you forget, you may be celebrating your next one *alone.*

A homemade scrapbook. Create a history of your life together. Include photos and written materials from places you've been, things you've done together, etc. You can keep buying blank pages and add to the original, creating a set of volumes as the years go by.

536. A tape of the original version of "your song."

537. Your wedding photo (if you're not married, a special photo from the "early days")—in a frame engraved with the date and occasion.

538. An oil painting made from a cherished photo of your loved one or the two of you together.

539. A gold or silver charm of the number of years being celebrated.
Barbara had been collecting charms for her bracelet since childhood. Frank had a jeweler design a gold number 5 for the couple's fifth anniversary, and he placed it on her bracelet before the two went out to celebrate. Barbara proudly jangled through dinner and dancing—and insists on wearing her bracelet for every romantic occasion and "date" with Frank.

540. An ornament for the Christmas tree (if the two of you celebrate). For example, a sleigh painted or engraved with "Vinnie and Danielle, Christmas 1996."

 A CD player to plug into the cigarette lighter outlet in the car.

542. Candles—lots and lots of them, in a musky or exotic scent. They make great mood lighting.

543. Pick out a complete ensemble that you think your mate will look terrific wearing. Whether it's black leather or blue pinstripes—and whether it's ever worn in public—is irrelevant.

544. A stuffed animal.

 Great for a new relationship: A basket filled with a few items relating what you may know about the person so far.

Cynthia and Peter had just begun dating when Peter's 30th birthday came up. Cynthia gave him a card (not too mushy) and a basket filled with little knickknacks representing things that she had learned about him from their conversations so far. For example, Peter played golf and tennis, so Cynthia included a set of tees and a can of tennis balls. He also liked to read, so a nice bookmark was inside a paperback book. Cynthia finished off the basket by painting wooden initials and gluing them to the side of the basket, wrapping it all in colored cellophane and tying it with ribbon. Peter was so thrilled with the thoughtfulness of the gift, he showed it to everyone at work and even told his mom about it!

546. Wrap separate gifts following one theme, such as movies (videos, VCR, popcorn maker), music (CDs, songbooks, karaoke machine), personal indulgences (bath oils, perfumes, aftershaves), a sport (hockey sticks, hockey jersey, video of hockey bloopers, book about a famous hockey star) or a hobby (gardening tools, seeds, gardening guidebook or video).

Spending time together

Who says that every gift has to be wrapped? What about spending some time together? Dote on your significant other for an entire day, an evening or a few stolen hours. These are gifts that don't need a special occasion for giving. They're a great way to enrich a relationship anytime.

 A night in one of those "theme" rooms at a hotel. Choose from "Arabian Nights," "Tropical Passion" or a number of other fantasies. Call around to see what the area hotels offer.

548. A dinner cruise.

549. Tickets for a concert.

550. Rent an expensive car for the day (a Lamborghini, Porsche, etc.). Drive through the countryside or run errands—whatever would make your mate happy.

 A hot-air balloon ride (spring for champagne, too).

552. A ride on a bicycle built for two or a bike ride together on individual bikes. Choose roads that are a bit off the beaten path for a more romantic atmosphere. Maybe you can bring along a blanket and some wine and cheese.

553. A horse-and-carriage ride. Most major metropolitan areas feature these in attractive downtown areas.

554. A limousine ride for a tour of a nearby city.

 Commit to spending time doing something he/she loves but you hate—whether it's freezing your tush off at a football game, slapping yourself awake during an opera or having the in-laws over for dinner.

556. A day at a museum.

Spending time together

 A day of hiking or leisurely walking through a park or small town that neither of you is familiar with. Bring a picnic lunch or dinner.

558. A winetasting class.

559. Buy—don't rent—a favorite romantic movie that has some meaning for the two of you. Whether it's *Casablanca* (you love acting out your favorite parts of the script) or *When Harry Met Sally* (ditto...especially the restaurant scene), it's probably a good idea to have this film in your personal library. Schedule an evening the two of you can curl up on the couch with a bowl of popcorn...or a bottle of champagne.

560. Membership to a museum in the area would be appreciated if your "other" is a science or art fanatic. Membership probably includes special access privileges, guest passes or discounts.

561. A session (or several) with a personal trainer.
    Warning: This should not be attempted unless the relationship is pretty secure. If your significant other has expressed a desire to get in shape, this gift will be appreciated. If nothing's been said, your gesture could be misunderstood as personal criticism.

562. A foot care kit including a pumice stone, foot lotions, etc. Present a certificate for a foot massage/pedicure using the items you've bought.

563. Satin sheet set. It's a romantic gift, as well as a true indulgence. If he or she is bashful, no one has to know about them as long as they're covered up with a comforter. For the bold individual, include a great big satin comforter.

 A locket with your picture inside.

Unmentionables

Sexy underwear, of course, makes a great gift—one that can be enjoyed by both of you. But there's a caveat here. Be sure you know your "other" well enough that you are assured that the item will fit. This gift could backfire if your sweetie doesn't quite fill up that peek-a-boo bra or Mr. Studmuffin looks like a stuffed muffin in those spandex briefs. (See Appendix 1 for information on the Victoria's Secret catalog, a great source of lingerie for women.)

565. For her: bikini underwear.

566. For him: flannel boxers.

567. For her: a garter belt with stockings.

568. For him: a smoking jacket.

569. For her: a terry cloth robe and something satiny.

570. For her: a slinky slip.

571. For both: matching lingerie. After all, you're celebrating your togetherness on this special day.

572. Caviar, oysters or your sweetie's favorite aphrodisiac—even if it's just sinfully rich hot chocolate with marshmallows.

573. A favorite romance-inspired painting or photograph, framed by you. Consider Picasso's "The Lovers." (For more ideas, see the section on "Love in art" wedding gifts on page 107.)

574. A night out with the boys for him, a night out with the girls for her. No nagging allowed.

Chapter 6

Some *friend*-ly advice on gift-giving

What makes friends so much easier to buy for than parents, kids, teenagers or even significant others? They're your friends—which most often means that they're a lot like you. You know their tastes, their preferences—perhaps even what they have and don't have. And more so with your good friends than with anyone else, the strategy of giving them what *you'd* like to receive is one that usually leads to *oohs*, *ahhhs* and "You always know just what I want!"

One great gift-giving tactic to employ with friends? Take them out! What better gift than an evening at the theater/ballpark/movies with one of their favorite people? Make reservations at a favorite restaurant, plan a day at an amusement park or schedule an afternoon of spas, massages and manicures with your friend. The advantage to this strategy is that *you* get to enjoy the gift, too!

Be warned, however: Giving to friends can have its challenges. There are so many gift-giving occasions—covered specifically in this chapter are birthdays, weddings, baby showers and housewarmings. But there are also holidays, anniversaries, going-aways, get wells, retirements and endless situations in which a gift may be called for. Because you want to please or impress your friend with "just the right gift," it may be hard to come up with something special time after time. Perhaps the two of you even have a creative rivalry going. You may feel obligated to "top" the last gift you gave your friend—or the one your friend gave *you*.

Our advice is this: Relax, take a deep breath and have some fun with this gift recipient. There are so many possibilities ahead of you, and we present more than 200 to choose from here.

 Flowers are always a great gift, whether you have an arrangement delivered to the home or workplace, or whether you arrive at the door with a fragrant bouquet.

576. A funny book to cheer up a friend. Jerry Seinfeld's *SeinLanguage*, Tim Allen's *Don't Stand Too Close to a Naked Man* or one of David Letterman's books of "top ten" lists should tickle a funny bone.

577. A bestseller or two on tape. Especially good for your busy friends who travel frequently or have long commutes.

578. In any shape or size, a clock is always a "timeless" gift. Croll Clocks in Hackensack, N.J., makes clocks with names, dates, events, etc., engraved on them. You can reach the company at 201-484-5781.

579. A night at a comedy club to see a favorite comedian.

580. A big, sturdy umbrella. We all probably have two or three umbrellas in various stages of disrepair. Every time it rains, we have to try to remember which has the broken handle, which has the spoke popping through and which is barely large enough to cover our shoulders. When it comes to these occasionally used necessities, few of us are willing to invest in the high-quality stuff. A good umbrella, though practical, will be a much appreciated gift.

 Sign up a single friend for a dating service. Seems a little risky, but more often than not, it ends up being appreciated. Most of the time, the person may have been thinking about signing up, but just wasn't motivated to do so.

Several years ago, Katherine's brother signed her up for a local dating service as a birthday present. She was annoyed at first, uncomfortable with the idea of being paired up with "strange men." But since she wasn't dating anyone at the time, she reluctantly agreed to give it a try. The third man she dated is now her husband—and the father of her darling baby boy!

Inexpensive

If you've got a lot of love in your heart, but not a lot of money in your wallet, here are some inexpensive, yet thoughtful, gifts— some of which you can make yourself.

 A tape of your friend's favorite CD selections. You can classify it "The Best of '96," "Howard's Favorites from the '90s" or selections from the recipient's favorite music genre. Your entire investment is time and the cost of a high-quality cassette tape. Add a personally designed tape jacket for that extra touch.

583. Lottery tickets when the stakes are big.

 A coupon book, offering to take care of kids/pets while your friend is away, a full day of shopping or fishing together, a girls'/guys' night out, etc.

585. A humorous video starring your friend. Add his or her favorite songs for a soundtrack.

 A wooden plaque with mementos or souvenirs from an excursion you spent with your friend (drink coasters or napkins, matchbook covers, theater/concert tickets, photos, party invitations, etc.) shellacked onto it.

587. A small photo album highlighting a celebration, vacation or occasion you spent together: Recapture the frenzy and foolishness of your friend's move-in day, preserve the feelings of camaraderie at your co-worker's going-away party.

 A framed painting or drawing you did yourself.

589. Corporate stocks. They don't have to be "blue chips," just a few shares in a company that makes one of your friend's favorite products—No More Frizzies shampoo, Crunchy Critters cereal. Be creative.

590. A stuffed animal. No matter what their age, most people enjoy the warmth and softness of a stuffed animal from a special friend or group of friends.

    For her birthday, two of Rachel's friends jointly gave her a giant stuffed bear jammed into a tiny box that exploded as soon as she removed the tape from the sides. After seven years, Rachel still has the bear, "Journey" (named after Jon and Bernie, the two who gave it to her), and she'll always remember the way she felt when it first jumped out at her.

 "Worry people." A Guatemalan folklore gift—a sack of tiny dolls made of wire and cloth. Tradition has it that you assign a trouble to each doll, put them back in the sack and they "take care" of your problems. They're cute, colorful—and cheaper than a therapist.

592. A demitasse set—great for entertaining friends or enjoying a break during the day.

 An "Eye of the Storm," a glass sphere with lightning dancing around inside.

594. A tropical "beach party in a bucket."

    Judy put one together for her sister's May birthday. She bought an acrylic ice bucket, which was decorated with a colorful fish motif, and filled it with a few reusable ice cubes shaped like fish and shells, palm-tree-shaped swizzle sticks, plastic goblets with sea horse stems, a couple of cocktail mixes, some brightly colored citronella candle torches—even a Jimmy Buffet tape. Because Judy's sister was renting a beach house that summer, it was a gift that was "shore" to please!

For female friends

Stumped about what to get fussy Cousin Edna for her birthday? Pulling your hair out about a gift for the woman who has everything? Try these:

595. A daily skin-care regimen from a big-name cosmetics company. Include products such as eye cream, night cream, alpha hydroxy lotion, cleanser, toner, foundation—tailored to the person's skin type. A promotional tote bag or other bonus is usually included at no charge if you spend enough money.

596. A fancy compact.

 A floral-patterned lipstick case.

598. A new set of makeup brushes.

599. A perfume sprayer.

600. Bath oil that comes in a decorative, tinted bottle with rose petals or something botanical floating inside.

601. Body wash, sponge, shower pouf or loofah, fragrant soaps, bath crystals, powder, lotion, etc. A miscellaneous assortment put together in a basket or decorated box is always a nice gift.

602. A lighted makeup mirror.

603. Solid perfume in a porcelain gift box.

604. A charm bracelet. Supply the first charm—one half of one of those "best friends" broken hearts is a nice beginning.

For female friends

 A friendship ring. Choose a ring with both of your birthstones or consider a Claddagh ring, an Irish symbol of love and friendship.

606. A gold charm with your friend's college name or logo. It can be worn on a charm bracelet or a necklace.

607. A makeover. Often, these are free at department store makeup counters. But you can schedule an appointment for a friend, and include a gift certificate for a cosmetics purchase.

608. How about a T-shirt and mug from the TV show *Friends*? You can find these items at various stores, including the Warner Brothers store in your local mall, or through catalogs, such as Signals (see Appendix 1).

609. Aromatherapy candles or incense—for example, a lavender-scented candle to help induce sleep.

610. A singing telegram. You can choose from all manner of costumed entertainers, including bears, clowns, cartoon and movie characters. For the wild and crazy, there's also a strip-o-gram.

 A portable CD player. Like a book on tape, this is good for the commuter or frequent traveler.

612. Vacation souvenirs. When you go away, bring back something native to the area where you bought it, not something that you could pick up just as easily at your local Kmart. Your friend can live vicariously through the object. It can be functional, too, such as a handwoven scarf from Greece or a tea towel from Ireland.

613. A big, bowl-style, pottery coffee mug.

For male friends

Your best bud just got that new job he's been after…your nephew is celebrating his 30th birthday…your brother is graduating from law school. You want to get something special, but what? Men can be tough to buy for, whether you're a woman or another man. Here are some ideas that may be appropriate for your situation. Also, be sure to read Chapters 7 and 8 for more ideas.

614. Cuff links or a tie tack engraved with his initials.

615. A game ball signed by a favorite player.

616. An ID bracelet with his name on it.

617. Desk accessories, including blotter, pen/pencil holder, calendar, Rolodex and organizer.

618. A bottle of cologne.

    Matt decided to venture into the stock market by buying some shares in a well-known company. Shortly afterwards, for Matt's birthday, his co-worker, Louise, gave him a bottle of Preferred Stock cologne—a clever combination of timing and finding an appropriate product name.

619. A tie with a fun or funky design on it.

 A satellite package to watch his favorite sports team outside of his city.

621. A case of exotic beer (if he drinks it) and a mug.

622. A good pen set.

623. An engraved brass calling card case. Some come with built-in calculators.

Lessons

There are plenty of continuing education classes at local colleges and high schools, where a variety of studies are offered. Classes tend to last just a few weeks and tuition is minimal. Check out a schedule, and let these ideas stimulate your imagination:

624. A class on a specific software program for the new computer owner who keeps pestering *you* for help.

625. A crash course in a language. Italian for the friend who's planning a trip to Italy next winter. Beginning Japanese for a co-worker who is scheduled to visit overseas clients in a few months.

626. A financial planning class for the friend who has become interested in investing.

627. A vegetarian cuisine class for someone who just swore off meat.

628. Specialty cooking lessons (Thai, Italian, nouvelle, whatever).

629. Your neighbor just invested in a fancy-schmancy camera? Sign him or her up for some photography lessons.

630. A yoga class.

631. A winetasting class. (Supply a bottle of good wine for the homework assignments!)

632. Ballroom, jazz or tap dancing lessons.

 A full season of tennis lessons.

634. Country line dancing lessons. Then get your friend to teach *you* the dances, and y'all can go out and kick up your heels together.

635. A game. Consider a fancy deck of cards with matching scorecards, or Pictionary, Scrabble, Trivial Pursuit, Monopoly, Twister, Scruples, Uno, etc.

636. A gift certificate for a store that specializes in unusual games.

637. Personalized playing cards, chips and an automatic card-shuffler.

638. *The New Complete Hoyles: The Official Rules of All Popular Games* by Edmond Hoyles.

639. A sturdy card table and chairs. Great for "bridge night" or for extra seating at holiday meals.

 For the true couch potato, a TV mood video. You just insert the tape...and stare at tropical fish, a burning fire or ocean waves on your TV screen. (See the Johnson Smith catalog in Appendix 1.)

641. Pencils, pens and notepads with the recipient's name on them (especially if he or she is a student or writer).

642. A universal remote. If the electronics buff has lots of remotes for many electronic devices, it will solve the problem of misplacing one.

 Handmade postcards, notepaper or personalized letterhead—if you're adept at desktop publishing (or if you know someone you can hire).
On Jane's spring break trip to New Orleans with her best friend and college roommate, Heather, she was disturbed to find that the all-you-can-eat shrimp still had their heads and eyes intact. Months later, Heather made Jane postcards that had a shrimp on the front (head and eyes included) with a "no" symbol through it. No one else understood the stationery without an explanation (except for the spring break crew), but to Jane, it was hilarious.

644. For a bookworm friend, a hardcover edition of a current bestseller.

645. A subscription to a magazine or newspaper (vocational, religious, hobby, etc.). Buy the current issue and give it to the recipient with a note explaining that more issues will be coming for a year.

646. A car emergency kit, including jumper cables, flares, first aid supplies, etc. Great for someone with a new car.

647. A professional massage.

648. A manicure or pedicure at a favorite or exclusive salon.

 Home office supplies. Notepads, roll tape, printer/copier paper, paper clips, rubber bands, sticky notes, pens, pencils, correction fluid, labels, etc. Use your imagination to create a gift basket— maybe fill a new storage bin or wastebasket with these items.

650. A personalized bottle of wine.

For the 25th wedding anniversary of her friends Howard and Marilyn, Alexandra ordered a case of wine from a wine magazine. The bottles had personalized labels saying, "Howard and Marilyn's 25th Wedding Anniversary." Alexandra added a crystal bottle coaster to complete the gift idea. Now that's class!

651. A self-help book or a book of daily affirmations or meditations.

Special occasions

Birthday

This is a great time to show your friend how happy you are that he or she is alive! Here are some ideas for celebrating the person's birthday in a special way.

652. A birthday-gram with balloons.

 Bake your friend a cake. Go all out with the decorations.

654. A book that focuses on the date or year your friend was born, including all the notable facts, events and personalities of the time. You can usually find these types of books in card stores.

655. Plan and throw a big, elaborate surprise party. Although parties are not usually considered gifts in themselves, all of your hard work—contacting friends and relatives, coordinating music, decorations and food *and* trying to keep it all a secret—may very well represent one of the best gifts your friend has ever received.

 A newsletter created by you! Incorporate your friend's name into the newsletter's title. Each story is related to the person's life, the people in his or her life, etc. Each headline describes a milestone (go for humor). One story can be about his or her birthday. Have the newsletter printed up, put it in a plastic bag and place it on your friend's front porch. You can also deliver it to your friend's friends and family, so they all can read about the birthday. (Perhaps include a story about a party for the person if you're planning to have one.)

Housewarming

It's not really *houses* you're warming, it's *people*! Make your friends feel at home by giving gifts that comfort or remind them of something familiar.

657. A fancy corkscrew and a bottle of wine. Too many people use Swiss army knives to open good bottles of wine!

658. If you're artistic or familiar with desktop publishing, make up "new address" cards. If you're not, have them professionally printed.

659. A decorative or custom-made personalized mailbox.

 A box of recipes. Include your favorite recipes (or faves you collected from others), neatly written (perhaps accompanied by colorful illustrations) on unlined, white index cards. Place in a nice recipe box or one you designed.

661. A wine rack.

662. A bar set including a shaker glass, strainer, tin shakers, ice scoop, bar spoon and bottle top pourers.

663. A day of cleaning—by a professional cleaning service—for your friend's home.

664. A basket filled with a phone message pad, pens and a couple of prepaid phone cards.

665. A decorative phone.

666. A boot scraper, which may resemble a prickly porcupine. It's great for scraping off all that mud that gets caught in the soles of athletic shoes and always seems to loosen up on carpet.

667. A dustbuster. Most people already have a vacuum, but these little cleaners come in handy for quick pickups.

 A birdhouse-replica of your friend's house. Whether *you* make it or pay someone else to, it's sure to please a nature-loving friend.

669. A gift certificate to a curtain/shades store or a home/garden center.

670. A bagel slicer for the bagel-lover. Resembling a guillotine, it slices through the bagel with ease.

671. A decorative teapot.

672. A heated towel rack for the bathroom.

673. A laundry basket, drain board or plastic basin filled with cleaning items and/or miscellaneous utensils.

674. A house marker with the family's name on it. It can be posted right on the house, attached to the mailbox or "planted" into the lawn.

675. A house number plaque, available in a wide variety of styles. Few new homeowners remember to put this on their shopping list. It's a nice gesture at a reasonable price.

676. An electric broom. Great for cleaning wood or tile floors.

677. A spice rack stocked with spices in matching containers.

678. Oil and vinegar in tinted, decorative bottles with herbs suspended inside (sage, basil, rosemary). (*Buy* it this way; don't try to make it yourself. Research has shown that the oil can carry bacteria if you don't do it properly.)

 Vases with artificial plants or flowers (some look pretty real). The best are the ones you design and make yourself.

680. A fireplace set. These usually include a poker, shovel, brush, log lifter and stand. Also consider other fireplace accessories—a decorative damper, a basket of color-treated pine cones or a brass cricket. ("Crickets on the hearth" are traditionally believed to bring good luck.)

681. A set of Rubbermaid-type storage containers.

682. A sake set, consisting of four small cups and a pitcher (usually ceramic), traditionally used for serving Japanese rice wine. This makes a unique gift for someone who is not Asian-American, and using it can become a tradition between you and the recipient.

683. A pot rack that hangs on the wall, creating more space in the kitchen.

 A liquid soap dispenser for the kitchen sink. These are offered in ceramic, crystal and plastic. Try to match it with your friend's kitchen design.

685. A personalized welcome mat.

A carton of light bulbs...in every size and wattage.
When Ellen and Leo bought their first home, Uncle Ralph gave them a large box of every size and type of light bulb imaginable—outdoor lights, refrigerator light bulbs, chandelier bulbs. While they initially laughed about the gift and chalked it up to Ralph's eccentricity, they grew to appreciate the thoughtfulness of the gift. Especially since they didn't have to buy a light bulb for years!

687. An herb- or flower-growing garden for the kitchen window.

688. A lamp—whether brass, crystal, iron, ceramic, Tiffany-style, Victorian, antique or torchiere halogen, there are lots of ways to light up someone's life.

689. A wheelbarrow filled with a garden hose, watering can, gloves and gardening tools.

 A gas grill; some sets come with all the necessary utensils.

691. A set of barbecue tools and a chef's hat.

692. A set of backyard picnic accessories, such as plastic plates, tumblers and utensils, a picnic table cover and a citronella candle.

693. A decorative outdoor flag (don't forget the flagpole and bracket, if your friend doesn't have them).

694. A lawn game, such as a croquet, horseshoes or volleyball/ badminton set.

695. An outdoor thermometer. They make some really fancy designer ones these days. L.L. Bean has some attractive thermometers in brass. (See Appendix 1.)

696. A brass fixture for an outdoor faucet.

697. Garden decorations—terra cotta bunnies, a verdigris sundial or turtle.

698. A planter box for the porch railing.

699. A quilt or throw for a rocking chair.

700. A perpetual calendar made out of wood, consisting of interchangeable blocks with the dates on them. There are also blocks with icons for special holidays.

 A set of plates you bought and decorated (with nontoxic paint) yourself.

702. Small, decorated wooden furniture, such as a kitchen or bedroom chest, potato and onion bin, shadow box, trash bin, etc. You can find these, finished and unfinished, at craft shows and craft/woodworking stores. Add a special touch by decorating and finishing them *yourself.*

703. A bread warmer. It's a ceramic dish you heat up in the oven, cover with a dishcloth and place just-baked bread upon to keep it warm.

704. A book of home remedies or hints on using household items to solve problems like stains on furniture or gum stuck in hair.

705. A uniquely shaped cookie jar.

 A stencil kit for decorating walls, furniture, floors, ceilings, etc.

707. A draft blocker. Resembling either an elongated animal or a whimsical person with long arms, this is placed at the bottom of a door to keep out cold drafts.

Hostess gifts

The list of "keep handy" gifts that appears in Chapter 1 is an ideal place to start when considering a gift for the person who's invited you to a party or holiday dinner or hosting you for a weekend visit. Also, food or food baskets are considerations. Here are a few additional ideas:

 A potpourri burner or jar or a basket of loose potpourri.

709. A decoration for the door.

710. A centerpiece.

711. Decorative or fragrant candles.

 A soap dish with colored, scented soaps inside.

Engagement and bridal shower gifts

Many items can be given as *either* engagement, bridal shower or wedding gifts, while others, because of practicality or tradition, are distinctly pre-wedding. Here are a few:

713. A wedding organizer file. This usually comes in a decorative file box and is an excellent way to keep track of all the details of planning a wedding.

 A gift certificate for wedding photography.

715. Items for the reception: a cake topper, silver cake server or monogrammed champagne glasses.

716. A certificate for a facial, massage, etc., to relieve nerves before the wedding.

717. For a warm-weather honeymoon, buy a beach bag and fill it with various strengths of sunblock, after-sun lotion, moisturizer, a beach blanket, beach towels, sunglasses, water shoes, a Frisbee, a beach ball, a water bottle, etc.

718. A certificate for some pre-honeymoon tanning sessions.

719. Bridal magazines give helpful hints on the wedding process and contain plenty of advertisements for bridal and attendants' gowns. Start a subscription for your friend.
Gloria and her brother, John Paul, each bought a subscription for John Paul's bride-to-be after the engagement announcement. She chose her wedding gown from one of the issues.

720. A wedding planning book. Every couple planning a wedding can use a guide to help them with the "big day" details. Try *The Best Wedding Ever* and *The Complete Book of Wedding Vows* by Diane Warner.

 If you have good handwriting, volunteer to do the calligraphy for the wedding invitations. In some metropolitan areas, this typically costs $2.50 an envelope. Your help will be greatly appreciated.

Wedding

Money, of course, is a universally accepted wedding gift. Also, most couples are registered at one or more major department stores. This allows gift-givers to learn exactly what the couple would like to receive. However, your budget may be limited, making a gift of money or a place setting of Royal Doulton china a financial difficulty. Here are some gift ideas, many that would be acceptable as bridal shower or engagement gifts, as well.

722. A breakfast-in-bed ensemble. One or two nice trays, attractive cloth napkins, coffee cups and saucers, plus gourmet coffee beans, muffins or jam.

723. A hefty cookbook, such as *The New York Times Cookbook*, or even a selection of smaller books—including Chinese, Italian, vegetarian, barbecuing—or whatever is appropriate to the tastes of the couple.

 The *Special Effects Cookbook* for some eye-opening recipes. The lucky couple can create exploding volcano cakes and other edible catastrophes. This book can be ordered from Miles Kimball (see Appendix 1).

725. A "prosperity tree"—a wire tree in a marble base, decorated with tiny bells, said to bring luck and prosperity to the recipient.

 Mount and shellac the wedding invitation for a beautiful keepsake.

A video camera and tapes.

728. A basket of gourmet foods and unusual cooking supplies. (See Chapter 8 for food-related gifts.)

729. A gift certificate for a supermarket to help get them started with the basics.

730. Cooking lessons, for one or both of them together, especially if it's the first time either will need to cook family meals.

 A wedding time capsule. A metal box or canister that contains a book to record memories and facts from the first year of marriage and enough space to hold keepsakes—everything from the marriage certificate to photos from the wedding to love letters sent between the two.

732. A picnic basket with supplies inside—for those romantic newlywed outings. Include cloth napkins, flatware, plates and cups, wine glasses, wine bottle opener, red and white checker cloth to spread on the ground, food storage containers, etc.

733. For Jewish couples, a Lenox mezuzah will make them feel established and blessed in their new home.

 If the couple is married in a traditional Jewish ceremony, you can have the broken glass (stepped on by the groom) preserved in Lucite.

735. A personalized throw blanket embroidered with the couple's names and wedding date.

 Design letterhead and envelopes personalized with the couple's names and address, and have them professionally printed.

737. A brass door knocker with their names engraved on it.

738. His and hers monogrammed bathrobes.

After the wedding, take the centerpiece from the table you're sitting at, hang the flowers to dry, press them and layer them by color in a uniquely shaped glass bottle.

740. For the bride, a trousseau—a nightgown, robe or other lingerie to wear on her wedding night.

 A neighborhood swimming pool membership. It'll be a good way for the couple to meet people from the community.

742. First-night-back dinner. Have an entire dinner delivered to the couple's home when they return from their honeymoon.

Love in art

743. "The Wedding" by Marc Chagall.

744. Picasso's "The Lovers."

745. Grant Wood's "American Gothic."

746. A pewter or brass replica of Robert Indiana's "LOVE" sculpture.

Baby shower/gifts for new parents

Let's face it. When we're talking new baby gifts, we're really talking *new parent* gifts. Those cute little rompers are outgrown in a month. And a newborn is not going to appreciate those numerous crib toys and rattles. So focus on "keepsake" items—something the infant will hold special as an older child, even as an adult. (For gifts that babies and toddlers will enjoy or play with, see Chapter 3.) Or give something the parents will appreciate now. Consider some of the following:

747. A baby monitor, to be within earshot of the baby at all times. Similar to a walkie-talkie system.

748. A baby/toddler gate.

749. A diaper disposal unit.

750. A stroller.

 A baby jogger. This is a stroller designed specifically for pushing at a fast speed, while running or jogging. For a parent who jogs regularly, so he or she won't have to give it up.

752. A car seat.

753. A baby carrier.

754. An exersaucer. Used in place of a walker—it excercises the leg muscles, without the mobility of a walker, making it safer.

755. A swing. Either a wind-up one or a battery-operated one. These are great for soothing a fussy baby and will be greatly appreciated by any parent.

756. A basket full of all the baby care essentials new parents will need to keep baby healthy and happy: diapers, baby powder, baby oil, diaper rash lotion, bottles, diaper changing pad, baby aspirin, thermometer, wipes, etc.

757. A crib blanket and linens.

 A decorated container to serve as a catch-all near the changing table. Also a nice keepsake.

Sally painted a large flower pot with pastel colors, then pasted the baby's birth announcement as well as colorful photos and whimsical pictures cut out of magazines. She presented it to the new parents who cherished it so much, they continued using it as a mail holder long after their baby outgrew diapers.

759. Books on general advice. Try *What to Expect in the First Year* by Arlene Eisenberg, Heidi E. Murkoff and Sandee E. Hathaway, RN.

 A book on how to massage a baby, along with the recommended oils. (It's supposed to be terrific for the baby.)

761. A gift certificate for new clothes for the mother *after* the baby is born.

 An engraved silver cup or tiny hairbrush set are traditional gifts. Expensive, yes, but classy and keepsake.

763. A "parents' night out." Dinner for two at a romantic restaurant—plus, offer to baby-sit while the parents are out.

764. A coupon book for baby-sitting. For example, include 10 coupons, each good for one evening of baby-sitting—by you.

765. A subscription to a parenting magazine. Most new parents are avid readers of parenting literature. A year's subscription will keep them poring through the latest topics and tips.

766. For the environmentally correct, a subscription to a diaper service (for a few months or a year).

 A complete astrological reading of the new baby. Individuals who provide this service often use a computer program. The baby's date and time of birth are input and out comes a detailed reading of the infant's future, based on the movement of his or her sun sign. Two points to keep in mind: Be sure the parents will get a kick out of this sort of thing, and make sure that there isn't a focus or interpretation on anything too negative or scary.

 A crocheted baby carriage cover. This is a typical grandma gift. It can become an heirloom with proper care.

769. If you're a photographer, offer to do a portrait session for baby once he or she is old enough to do something cute. Be forewarned: This may turn out to be an expensive gift, especially if you're covering all development costs. New parents are notorious for photo overkill and will probably want a zillion copies of every pose.

770. A baby-wipe warmer. Yes, such a thing really does exist.

771. A gift certificate to a baby specialty store. Don't overlook, however, a gift certificate to a grocery or drugstore. New parents are always running out to stock up on diapers, formula and cotton swabs.

772. A vibrating baby pad to calm fussy infants.

773. Videos for passing sleepless nights. New parents will probably not see a night out for quite a while. New movies or old favorites will be much appreciated. Consider parent-theme movies, from classics such as *Cheaper by the Dozen* and *The Parent Trap*, to the more recent *Parenthood.* If you're feeling particularly perverse, consider *Mommy Dearest* or *Serial Mom.*

774. Savings bonds. By the time the child is old enough to appreciate your gift, the bond itself will probably have appreciated to twice the current value!

775. Stock in a reputable company. Hopefully it'll grow with the child.

776. A coin set from baby's birth year. It will only increase in value.

777. A food processor and a book on how to make homemade baby food. It's much healthier than canned and jarred food.

778. A child's room lamp. These are colorful theme lamps, such as sports or animals, etc. Maybe you can find one to match the decor of the new baby's nursery.

 A mounted and shellacked baby announcement.

780. A tiny silver spoon and supply of various baby foods. (The spoon is a good start to a collection you can help the child make over his or her lifetime.)

 For baby's first birthday, have the baby's first pair of shoes bronzed.

A baby time capsule. A decorative box or canister containing the following: a scrapbook and baby's history book to record facts, dates and memories (such as first word spoken, first steps, etc.); a photo album; a baggie for a lock of hair; space for any type of memorabilia about baby's first years.

783. A tree or shrub planted in honor of the baby so they can grow together.

784. A handknit monogrammed afghan.

785. A bathtime kit: towels, bath toys, as well as gentle shampoos, bubble baths, creme rinses and liquid soaps. Assemble them all in a plastic baby tub or some other creative container.

786. A tiny lacy pillow with baby's name embroidered on it.

 A "Day You Were Born" scrapbook. Collect a couple of newspaper headline pages and a list of the top music hits from *Billboard* or *Rolling Stone*. Cut out colorful movie ads that are currently playing. Even include a tape of some songs from the radio, or a couple of goofy commercials. Sports scores, pictures from the fashion pages, even prices from the grocery ads and real estate listings will be fascinating fodder to read through when the infant grows up.

Chapter 7

"I gave at the office!" Gift ideas for co-workers

The authors recognize that many of you may actually like your co-workers and consider them friends. Thus, you'll want to refer to Chapter 6 for additional gift ideas. However, many of us must work alongside people we aren't particularly close to or don't necessarily socialize with outside of the occasional company picnic or department happy hour. Yet, we are still confronted with birthdays, weddings, promotions, retirements, holiday exchanges and other reasons to consider giving something to a fellow worker. Keeping in mind that we may be obliged to present a multitude of gifts to a plethora of people we don't know that well, most of the ideas in this section are career-oriented, nonpersonal and relatively inexpensive. The more expensive gifts—a leather briefcase, for example—make good departmental "pitch-in" gifts.

Don't let yourself get caught in awkward gift-giving situations in the office. Imagine that it's your assistant's last day, the boss's birthday, a co-worker's promotion or the department gift-exchange party—and you forgot! We advise keeping a small supply of emergency gifts as well as a stack of general occasion cards in a desk drawer just for such surprise situations. (Review Chapter 1 for a list of terrific "on-hand" gift ideas.)

Another problem: the holiday season. How do those who celebrate deal with those who *don't* celebrate and vice versa? In most office environments today, the holiday festivities don't take on a religious tone—so that those who don't observe Christmas may still be comfortable taking part in organized gift exchanges, although no one should be pressured to do so. Remember to be sensitive to differences.

Keep this in mind, also, if you're responsible for sending holiday greetings or gifts to clients or customers who may not celebrate Christmas. Keep the holiday message generic for those who might instead observe Chanukah, Kwanzaa or even winter solstice. Regarding gifts, more companies are doing away with the traditional fruitcake or sausage-and-cheese tray and, instead, donating to worthy causes in the name of the recipient. (A group donation is also a great alternative to exchanging gifts among co-workers.)

For those who do choose to participate in gift exchanges, and for all of the other gift-giving situations you're confronted with in the workplace, this chapter will offer you plenty of great gift ideas. But be sure to read Chapter 8 for a list of travel-related gifts for the businessperson on the go.

788.   A good leather binder that holds a pad and pen.

 A stylish briefcase.

790.   A gold monogrammed pen and pencil set.

791.   A monogrammed money clip.

792.   A monogrammed business card holder.

793.   A classy cover for a day planner, to replace the basic vinyl one planners usually come in.

794.   A desk calendar that's more interesting than the institutional variety. Maybe one of those tear-off "joke-of-the-day" jobs, or something with beautiful pictures that allow a mental escape from the confines of the office.

795.   A subscription to *The New York Times*, *The Wall Street Journal*, *Forbes* or another highly regarded newspaper or magazine.

 An electronic organizer/planner.

Coffee break

Coffee mugs are a traditional co-worker gift. But set yourself apart with these thoughtful ideas:

 A traveling coffee mug. Great for the commute to work.

798. An artsy-looking demitasse or cappuccino cup.

799. For the true coffee addict, an attractive carafe that will keep a multicup supply hot all morning.

800. A small, plug-in warmer that will keep a mug warm for the slow sipper.

801. Coasters for the worker who hosts others at his or her desk for morning meetings.

 A package of chocolate-dipped or candy-coated spoons for stirring yummy flavors, such as mocha, into a cup of coffee. Sold at many sweets shops.

803. A sampling of gourmet flavored coffees (make sure these are ground—not everyone owns a bean grinder), specialty teas or hot chocolate.

804. Sign up your co-worker with the Coffee Quest, a coffee-of-the-month service. Each month, he or she will receive 2 pounds of gourmet coffee and a newsletter, for $16.95 per month. (Call 800-854-2337.) You can sign up for as little as two months. This makes a great group gift.

 A "Do Not Disturb" sign for the frazzled worker who is constantly interrupted.

806. Personalized note paper ("From the desk of...") or stationery.

Desk toys

Desk toys make great gifts for fellow workers who, like you, probably suffer from brain drain and seek a diversion to restore their creative juices and enthusiasm.

807. A kaleidoscope. Select from inexpensive kid types to brass "executive" models on wooden pedestals.

808. An abacus. A great gift, especially for those who "crunch numbers." If you live in a major metropolitan area, you can find the real thing in a Chinatown, or look in specialty gift stores or catalogs.

809. A sculpture with tiny magnetized pieces of metal that you can form into shapes.

810. A face-sculpture made of straight pins. (It's a lot safer to use than the office copy machine!) You can find this at Brookstone (see Appendix 1) or other game and gadget stores.

 Real toys. Pack a plastic bucket with Silly Putty, bubbles in a bottle, a tiny Etch-a-Sketch, even a box of crayons.

812. A Working Girl Barbie.

813. A basketball net to attach to a trash can.

 A mirror—one that can be hung up on an office door or on the wall of a cubicle. In addition to enabling quick makeup or hair checks before important meetings, the mirror can be a helpful tool for those individuals who spend a lot of time on the phone. Any customer service or telemarketing professional will tell you how important it is to put a smile in your voice—even when others can't see you.

815.   A small picture frame to hold a cherished photo of a loved one.

 A customized picture frame. Buy a basic wood picture frame and decorate it. For children's pictures—around the edge of the frame glue on little cut-out colorful geometric designs or pieces from a favorite game (for example, pieces of Monopoly money and playing cards arranged into a collage on the frame edge). For newlyweds—glue on lace or ribbon, dried flowers, dried roses, baby's breath, etc.

817.   A great gift for the boss: a photo of the staff—a vintage black and white one with everyone dressed in Old West saloon attire.

818.   Decorative bookends. Department stores usually carry a selection of nontraditional bookends such as wooden "books" for someone in publishing, ornate "hole-in-one" trophies for the golf enthusiast or gavels on stands for those in the law profession.

819.   A desk lamp to shed a warmer light in the harsh glow of fluorescent overheads. Consider a Tiffany knock-off or a banker's lamp with a green shade.

820.   Desk organizers to match the personality of the individual— choose from country baskets, sleek black metal, clear Lucite, rustic wood and more.

821.   An insulated lunch cooler for those who bring their own. These range from simple bags to containers in crazy colors and shapes.

 Freshly baked cookies in a decorative tin.

823.   Movie tickets or certificate booklets.

824.   A personal paper shredder.

825.   For the computer user, a fun mouse pad.

Wardrobe accessories

For most working individuals, a professional-looking wardrobe and a polished appearance is as essential as a good attendance record. While buying a navy-blue suit may be going a little too far, you might consider these gift items to help your co-worker achieve that dressed-for-success image.

 Heel protectors for driving. For men or women, these small devices keep shoe heels in good condition even after months of daily commuting.

827. Cedar blocks or hangups for closets and drawers.

828. Scented drawer liners.

829. An automatic tie rack for men.

830. An earring tree for women.

831. A sturdy coat rack that stands or can hang on an office partition.

832. A monogrammed garment bag. Great for overnight business trips.

833. For men, the latest version of the "power tie."

834. For women, a silk scarf.

 For the truly paranoid, a telephone voice changer. This device will allow a co-worker to disguise his or her voice—to the opposite gender, to sound like a chipmunk or a robot.

836. A miniature vacuum cleaner for a computer keyboard.

Cheer up/de-stress

837. The "Happy Massager" by Tender Loving Things, Inc. These massagers, made from specially selected birch and maple trees, come in two different sizes. They are sturdy and guaranteed. Call 800-486-2896.

 If it's a co-worker you're particularly friendly with, leave a flower with an encouraging note on your co-worker's car windshield in the company parking lot. He or she will really appreciate it after a particularly difficult day on the job.

839. An hour-long professional massage.

840. De-stressing scents. Aromatherapy comes to the rescue with little bottles of fragrant oils. Chamomile or neroli to relax, for example, and bergamot or eucalyptus to revive. Get a frazzled co-worker a set—one to gear up for those hair-yanking meetings and the other to wind down. Found in many skin-care specialty stores, such as The Body Shop (see Appendix 1) and Bath and Body Works.

841. A tape or CD on relaxation, meditation or guided imagery.

842. Oriental stress reliever balls that you roll in your palm. These come in decorative boxes.

843. Screensaver or wallpaper for a person's computer. If you supply the photo, some photo processing places or computer supply stores can create wallpaper from a picture of the person, his or her loved one, pet or other favorite photo.

 A tip chart for calculating tips, for the frequent business traveler.

845. A stamp set for decorating stationery.

846. A book about the person's astrological sign and horoscopes for the year ahead. (Make sure the person is into this sort of stuff.)

 A stained-glass suncatcher. These come in all sorts of designs, so you can choose something of personal significance for the recipient.

848. Balloons...for whatever the occasion. Fill your workmate's cubicle or office with them.

849. An air cleaner for the cubicle office. (Great for those environments that aren't yet smoke-free!)

850. A gift certificate to a bookstore or an office supplies store.

851. A plant or tree (depending on space limitations) to give an office a "homey" look.

852. A basket or bag filled with scented items—hand lotions, lip balm and other items that your co-worker could employ on the job. These can be found at shops such as Crabtree & Evelyn and The Body Shop (see Appendix 1) for both women and men.

853. It's customary in many workplaces to take out the celebrant to a lunch. If this isn't a possibility because of shift or time limitations, a gift certificate for dinner, lunch or brunch for two is a nice alternative.

 An office-sized putting green with return.

855. Warm, fuzzy slippers to put on after taking off boots during the winter. This all depends on whether the atmosphere in the office is very (okay, *extremely*) relaxed.

856. A poster or framed picture for the co-worker's office.

857. An inspirational quote, framed and mounted for hanging.

858. A "nice" trash can instead of those black, industrial-type cans.

Books

Check the bookstore, an office supply store or even career catalogs for motivating books and cassettes to inspire your co-worker career-wise or even in personal life. Here are just a few:

859. *The Power of Positive Thinking* by Dr. Norman Vincent Peale.

860. *See You at the Top* by Zig Ziglar.

861. *Awaken the Giant Within* by Anthony Robbins.

862. *The Seven Habits of Highly Effective People* by Steven R. Covey.

863. *The Job Survival Instruction Book* and *How to Have All the Answers When the Questions Keep Changing* by Karin Ireland.

864. *100 Ways to Motivate Yourself* by Steve Chandler.

865. *What Color is Your Parachute?* by Richard Nelson Bolles.

866. *The Road Less Traveled* by M. Scott Peck.

Chapter 8

Gift recommendations for tons of avocations

Michelle, a collector of bovine memorabilia, says she's received enough cow-related gifts to open a museum. She has cow-patterned placemats, a cow-shaped milk pitcher, cow figurines, a cow cookie jar that moos when opened. Her sister even found her a cow costume—complete with udder—that she wears every Halloween. Even though her friends seem to have milked it for all it's worth, Michelle's cow collection continues to stimulate new and continually creative gift ideas—and, what's more, she loves every one of them.

Wealthy friend Jennifer can afford to—and *does*—buy anything she wants. Except, of course, the model-like figure she yearns for. She's a fitness fanatic who dedicates a good part of her life to pursuing new means of achieving the perfect body. Sure, she has more workout gear than Jane Fonda and a roomful of exercise machines that look like torture devices to you. But her avocation for fitness opens the door to numerous gift ideas that are sure to please her.

Lew has always created gift-giving challenges for family and friends. A guy with no hobbies or interests, he doesn't like to go out—whether to the movies, a museum or a sports event. He's not big on clothing, jewelry, games or music, and he has enough dietary limitations that food gifts are ruled out. Lew, however, travels a lot for his business. Long-distance drives, overnights in hotels and even some trips abroad generate a need for gadgets that make his commutes, flights and stays in unfamiliar places more comfortable. "Ahhh," his friends and family say with a sigh of relief, "Now, I know what to get Lew!"

Everyone—even the most difficult to buy for—pursues some hobby, pastime, unique personal activity or quirky interest you could easily indulge. Such special interests are the last bastion—and often the most productive—for the bewildered gift-giver. This is the chapter to turn to when you're looking for a very specialized gift for someone with a very specialized interest. We can only begin to tap the potential, however, and our list is certainly not all-inclusive. We merely provide a *taste* of the possibilities and advise you to use it as a springboard to other "theme" gift ideas.

For collectors

Dig deep enough and you'll discover that almost everyone collects something—even if they don't consider themselves collectors. For clues, just look around their personal abode. The refrigerator may be covered with magnets. The bookshelf may be cluttered with tomes on military strategy and autobiographies of generals. The bedroom of a feline fanatic is packed with pictures of cats, cat figurines, stuffed cats, earrings with cats, even kitty-covered sheets. A red-headed friend has a living room wall covered with pictures, carvings, wall-hangings and plaques featuring carrots.

The following is a *brief* list of some common and not-so-common collectibles to get you started.

867. Comic books.

868. Music boxes.

869. Stamps. Call 800-STAMP-24 for the latest collector series issued by the U.S. Postal Service.

870. Coins. Contact the U.S. Mint at 202-283-COIN for information on coin collecting and how to get started.

871. Autographs from celebrities.

872. Salt and pepper shakers.

873. 50s-era tin action toys. Choose from cars, robots, Godzilla and the like.

874. Authentic cartoon animation cels.

875. Autographed baseballs.

876. Baseball or other sports trading cards.

877. War memorabilia.

878. Collector's plates. Subjects include holidays, Coca-Cola, *Star Trek*, Elvis, cats and more.

879. Hummel figurines.

880. Old-fashioned tin signs, advertising everything from flowers, seeds and fruits to bottled beverages to classic automobiles to Route 66. These make whimsical decorations for the kitchen or den. A good source: Desperate Enterprises, Inc., in Medina, Ohio. Call 216-732-4859 for a catalog.

881. Animal figurines. Many people focus on a particular animal, such as frogs, pigs or dolphins. The more unusual, the more challenging—and fun—to try to find a new addition. One woman collects elephants but insists that the trunk be pointed upward. Another collects groundhogs—her menagerie includes everything from expensive crystal groundhogs to a groundhog boot scraper.

882. Thimbles.

883. Dolls.

884. Hats.

 Matchbooks from restaurants and nightclubs from around the world. (An easy and inexpensive gift to give—especially if you travel and entertain a lot.)

Refrigerator magnets.

887. Teddy bears.

Sue received what she calls one of her best gifts ever on Valentine's Day when she was 10 years old. Her family had just moved to a new state, halfway across the country. Everything seemed cold and strange. When she opened the gift from her parents and saw the whimsical white critter topped with a big, red bow, she suddenly felt warm and at home. It was the first teddy bear she'd ever gotten. She is now an avid collector and owns more than 50 bears.

888. College memorabilia. College bookstores are a great source for T-shirts, sweatshirts, blankets, throw rugs—even toilet paper—featuring the school crest and colors of a beloved alma mater.

Cultural gifts

Someone who appreciates the finer things in life will most likely go for any gift that acknowledges his or her supreme taste in or knowledge of art, music, literature, film and theater. (Check out Appendix 1 of this book for some great catalogs for ordering such gifts—specifically, the Wireless and Signals catalogs.) Keeping in mind that gifts don't always have to be something you can hold in your hands, here are some ideas for the cultured:

 Tickets to the symphony, ballet or a theatrical production. If you really want to splurge, give season tickets.

890. Membership to the closest major metropolitan museum. The person will be kept abreast of news about upcoming exhibits and can get discounts on shows and merchandise.

891. An out-of-print book or a rare edition of a book by a favorite author. Great for a bibliophile.

For art lovers

892. A coffee table book featuring the work of a famous artist, such as Monet, Picasso, Wyeth, etc. A major bookstore or museum gift shop will have plenty to choose from.

893. A day at an art gallery or art museum. Top it off with a box of note cards or a print of the masterpieces of Dali, Georgia O'Keeffe or a favorite artist from the museum gift shop.

 A coffee mug depicting Van Gogh, Matisse, Cezanne, etc. Also available from art museum gift shops.

895. For the artistically talented, try one or two of these: an art supply storage box, a smock, a drawing table with a lamp, pastels, brushes, mixing trays, paints, newsprint paper, tracing paper, a sketchbook, watercolors, rubber cement or eraser gum. Ott's is a good source of discount art supplies; call 800-356-3289 for a catalog.

For music lovers

896. An out-of-production vinyl record. You can thrill and impress someone by locating a long-lost favorite...but make sure he or she still has a phonograph.

897. A rare CD, cassette or album—something by an artist from another country, a special one-time recording, a rare dance-club mix of a well-known tune or an album from an artist whose music isn't very popular or mainstream—anything you have to order from one of those small music stores that specializes in rarities.

898. Membership to or sponsorship of a local public radio or TV station. During membership drives, stations often give away premiums such as CDs or videos. Sign the person up, and he or she will receive bulletins about special shows, as well as news about artists playing in the area.

Membership to the local symphony.

900. Hard-to-get tickets for a favorite recording artist's concert.

Denise never thought she'd get to see her idol Paul McCartney in concert—until her sister surprised her by giving her tickets for Christmas one year.

For movie buffs

901. A video or a video anthology such as the *Star Wars*, *Rocky* or *Friday the 13th* series of movies.

902. A gift certificate for a movie theater that shows the critically acclaimed, but often hard-to-find, foreign films with subtitles.

903. An original or reprint movie release poster. Rick's Movie Graphics, Gainesville, Fla., carries thousands of authentic film advertisement posters from as early as 1931 to the present. Call 800-252-0425 for a catalog.

Food/gourmet cooking

Think about how you can enhance the culinary life of someone you know who prides himself or herself as a gourmet cook or merely a food fanatic. Here's some food for thought:

904. A donut maker. How many people do *you* know who have one of these? Easy to use—donuts can be made with ingredients from around the house (flour, sugar, eggs) and flavored with virtually anything (bananas, strawberries, oats, raisins, cinnamon, etc.).

905. A ready-made tea party. On a nice serving tray, arrange two or three boxes of loose teas, a tea strainer, a box of shortbread or thin tea cookies, some tiny jars of jam, a jar of Devonshire cream and some scones.

906. A sampling of gourmet coffee beans, a grinder, a chocolate grater and some biscotti.

907. A selection of gourmet salsas, chili peppers and a good cookbook featuring Cajun, Southwestern or Mexican cuisine.

908. Two or three unusually flavored vinegars and oils in an attractive wooden salad bowl.

909. An ice-cream maker. Try Williams Sonoma for this and other gourmet foods and kitchen paraphernalia (see Appendix 1).

910. A big, decorated tin filled with two or three varieties of gourmet popcorn.

911. Cookie cutters and molds, baking ingredients and cookie toppings (sprinkles, candies, etc.)—all packed into a ceramic cookie jar.

912. Cooking lessons. Gourmet grocery stores, as well as adult education programs at community colleges, offer these.

 A decorative jar filled with pasta in various shapes and colors.

914. A pasta maker.

915. A dumpling press. The recipient can create a wide variety of *hors d'oeuvres*, side dishes and desserts, filled with potatoes, cheese, meat, fruit, jellies—anything the heart desires.

916. A notoriously good cheesecake. Every region of the country has its own "best" cheesecake, usually found for a whopping price in the freezer section of a gourmet grocery. Unless they're lactose-intolerant, most everyone appreciates this gift.

917. Gourmet deli carryout. A good gift for the noncook. Include some cheese, pâté and good bread, along with a bottle of wine.

 A clay or terra cotta jar for storing garlic cloves. It keeps them cool so they stay fresh.

919. Mail-order goodies. There *are* some items that won't win you many points—beware the party trays packed with processed cheese, sausage rolls and fruitcakes. However, a number of national specialty food stores offer an excellent array of gifts; Cheryl's Cookies and Crabtree & Evelyn are two.

920. A waffle iron. A variety of molds are available, including hearts, flowers, even cartoon characters.

921. A gourmet cookbook.

922. A grow-your-own-herbs-at-home kit. These come with a planter, soil and instructions. Or you could make one yourself by assembling some fancy pots and herb seeds.

 A day at a winery for winetasting and a tour.

924. A subscription to a gourmet cooking magazine, such as *Bon Apetit* or *Food & Wine*.

Fitness/sports/outdoors

If you know *for sure* that the gift recipient has an interest in fitness, outdoor recreation or a particular sport, try some of these ideas:

 Membership to a fitness club. Try to find one that offers a lot of options—tennis, racquetball, swimming, aerobics classes, etc.

926. A pedometer for the walking enthusiast.

927. A stepper (or two for stacking) for at-home step aerobics.

928. A portable cassette player with headphones or a headset radio to wear while exercising. These are available in sturdy, waterproof, sports models.

 Tapes to listen to on a portable cassette player while walking or exercising.

930. A glider. A unique way to work out, it's a floor mat for "gliding" upon from side to side in specially made shoes.

931. A session (or more) with a personal trainer.

932. A sweatband with a prestigious designer logo.

933. An appropriate workout video and a floor mat.

934. A water bottle in a strap to be worn around the waist or hung on the treadmill.

 If you really want to splurge, surprise the individual with a workout machine. Consider a rowing machine, stair climber, treadmill or stationary bike (you *can* get a decent one for less than $200).

936. Hand weights.

937. A sturdy, roomy gym bag.

938. A gift certificate to a sporting goods store.

 A weight or flex bench.

940. In-line skates and protective gear.

941. A diver's watch for the watersports enthusiast.

942. Light strap-on weights to be worn on ankles and wrists while jogging or walking.

943. A gift certificate to a health food store.

944. A heating pad, aspirin and Ben Gay for those times when he or she overdoes it.

For the cyclist:

945. A bike rack for the car.

946. A bike helmet.

947. A utility rack for carrying a backpack or other essentials on the back of a bike.

 A bike lock.

For hikers and outdoor lovers:

949. A leather fanny pack.

950. A sturdy but lightweight backpack.

951. A backpack cooler or soft, lightweight mini-cooler for snacks and drinks.

952. A water carrier. Check out the insulated water bag—it folds flat when empty—from Travelsmith for $32 (see Appendix 1).

953. A hammock to string up between trees for taking breaks.

954. A horseshoe set.

955. A day of whitewater rafting. Make sure to sign the person up for an appropriate skill level.

956. A mess kit.

957. A mini grill or stove.

958. A sleeping bag.

959. A small tent.

For travel

If you know the gift recipient is planning a world tour, a cross-country drive or a major move, or must commute often on the job, you can make his or her life easier with these thoughtful ideas.

 Luggage, of course. For the intrepid traveler who still schleps a bulky set of hardsided pieces, consider buying a couple of pieces of luggage with wheels built in.

961. A rolling garment bag.

962. A sturdy carry-on with lots of zippered pockets.

963. A lightweight luggage porter for the frequent traveler who *doesn't* want to give up the luggage without wheels.

 A travel version of the fog-free mirror.

965. A car document organizer for the glove compartment.

966. A good road atlas. Recommended: a compact version of a well-known, reliable atlas that will fit under the driver's seat or in the glove compartment.

967. A reliable travel alarm clock.

968. A hanging toiletry bag. Too often, hotel bathrooms have little counter space for personal items. A bag that conveniently hangs on a towel hook will free up some room.

969. Security money/document holders such as money belts, a neck wallet or passport pouch.

970. A travel health kit—create your own or purchase one from a travel catalog. A "world traveler" version can cost as much as $78. (See Appendix 1 for the Travelsmith catalog.)

971. Books on tape for long road trips.

972. A travel-size umbrella that fits under the car seat or in a suitcase.

973. For the overseas traveler, an electric currency adapter and the appropriate plug converters.

974. Membership to an auto road service. (If the individual already has a membership, you may be able to upgrade it to "plus" or "deluxe" status, offering a little more protection if there's a breakdown.)

 Sample-size travel products, including shampoo, lotions, toothpaste, aspirin, etc., in a toiletry bag.

976. Travel-size appliances, including irons, shavers, hair dryers and other hair paraphernalia.

977. A padded laptop-computer protector for the traveling businessperson. So sleek it can be slipped into your briefcase, it holds disks and other accessories.

978. A cushioned video camera cover.

979. A lead-lined film carrier for the avid photographer.

980. A currency conversion chart for an overseas traveler. Some calculators have built-in programs for converting dollars to the local currency.

981. A contoured fleece travel pillow for the car or airplane.

 Ear plugs and an eye mask to block out light for better rest during an overnight flight.

983. An auto air purifier that plugs into the lighter socket of a car.

984. How about donating your frequent flyer miles? You could give the person the benefits you would normally get—a certificate for an upgrade to first class or a free companion ticket, for example. Call your preferred airline to find out how.

For animal lovers or pet owners

 Present a certificate for the care and feeding of a beloved pet while he or she is out of town.

986. For a cat owner, a carpet-covered climbing "tree" or "condo" for the cat. It can cost anywhere between $25 and $200, depending on the size, but the recipient will surely appreciate it if it keeps Fluffy from tearing the furniture to shreds.

987. For a cat owner, a grow-your-own-catnip kit. Comes with seeds, soil and a cute planter (some are wooden or cat-shaped), and can be bought in a department store.

988. A donation to an animal protection service or an animal rights organization in the recipient's name.

989. A membership to the local zoo.

990. A subscription to a pet magazine, such as *Cat Fancy*.

Blasts from the past, kitsch collectibles and the truly tacky

There's no accounting for some people's tastes. They may *genuinely* admire the way those bright pink plastic flamingos glisten in the sun on their front porch. Or maybe they just get a kick out of watching bewildered houseguests pass through those long strands of beads that grace the entrance to their living room. In any case, when all else fails, resort to this list if for no other reason than to get a good laugh from the recipient. Some of the items here are nostalgic reminders and fab fads from the past. Others have always been tacky. But surprisingly, when given as gifts, these special mementos frequently take on a certain cachet, and their owners often display them proudly and defiantly.

 A mood ring, love beads or peace-symbol jewelry.

992. The *Saturday Night Fever* video or soundtrack or a CD of disco hits from the 70s.

993. An unforgettable recording by a one-hit wonder or something by an artist who's already seen his or her 15 minutes of fame. Consider anything by the Partridge Family, Tiny Tim, Sonny and Cher, the Archies—or William Shatner.

 Fuzzy dice for the rearview mirror.

995. A Hula-Hoop, a poodle skirt or some other 1950s memorabilia. A great source is Back to the 50s, in Las Vegas. For a catalog, call 800-224-1950.

996. A very large painting of Elvis Presley on a black, velvet background. If the recipient is not an Elvis fan, give a black-velvet matador instead.

 A gag bag—featuring a whoopie cushion, handshake-buzzer, chewing gum that turns teeth black, x-ray glasses and more.

998. A necktie with smiley faces—or *anything* with a smiley face, for that matter.

999. A Chia Pet or "sea monkeys"—for the friend who doesn't want the responsibility of a cat or a dog.

1,000. Something lovely for the front lawn—a yard jockey or a pair of pink flamingos, perhaps. The bigger and gaudier, the better.

1,001. Gold lamé clothing. Try undergarments for a real laugh!

Chapter 9

Wrapping
it up

Congratulations! You've found the perfect gift for co-worker Charlene's baby shower and you can once again concentrate on your work now that your gift-giving obligations have been fulfilled. Ahh, but you have one more important step before you're off the hook—you've got to wrap the thing. For those of us who are tape-dispenser-challenged, this may be no small feat. But if you dump your naked gift in Charlene's lap with no fanfare, we guarantee that, despite the impressiveness of the gift itself, her reaction will be less than enthusiastic.

If you're feeling lazy—and you have some leftover cash from your shopping excursion—you could simply have a department store gift-wrapping service take care of the dirty work for you. But there are lots of creative—and easy—options for appealing gift presentation that surpass traditional paper and ribbon. For example, you could put Charlene's gift in a diaper bucket and stick a bow on top. Or place it in a gift bag and put some colorful tissue inside.

The following ideas may be useful...but don't stop here. Give your imagination a workout!

✂ A gift basket is always a classy presentation when you're giving several small items. (Throughout this book, we have given many examples of gift basket assortments assembled in various ways.)

✂ A gift bag provides a lot of room for creativity—and it's often easier to put together than a wrapped gift.
For a friend's birthday, Lisa decided to go with a "cinema" theme. She bought an assortment of videos and put them in a black gift bag with silver foil gift liner. To complete the theme, she used actual videotape as ribbon to tie the bag handles together. (She happened to have a videotaped advertisement that a politician had mailed her during a campaign. The irony speaks for itself.)

✂ Use solid-colored tissue paper covered with stickers or glitter.

✂ Make "homemade" gift wrap by decorating plain brown or white rolled paper. You can use paints, stamp and ink, markers, cutouts, stickers or sparkles.
Artistic Bert cut open grocery bags and decorated them with his own drawings. Carlene and Jim cut out designs from scraps of leftover wrapping paper and then decorated white paper and a white bow with the cutouts.

✂ Instead of wrapping paper, wrap the gift in something connected to the gift or occasion. For example:
- The Sunday comics for a child's gift.
- Fabric for someone who sews (he or she can reuse the fabric).
- Wallpaper for a new home owner.
- Lace for a wedding couple.
- A map for a traveler.
- A baby blanket for a baby gift.

✂ For unusually large gifts, you can use either a decorated garbage bag or a paper tablecloth with a decorative pattern.

✄ Place the gift in a container that can be part of the gift. For example:

- A diaper bucket for a baby gift.
- A jewelry box for a small item.
- Homemade food in a casserole dish, freezer container or decorative holiday tin.
- A CD or cassette case for a musical recording.
- A small canvas lunch bag for a co-worker gift.

✄ Save pretty or unusual containers to be recycled as gift boxes. Many are attractive enough to stand without wrapping. Consider these:

- Fancy chocolate (Godiva's elegant gold, for example) boxes.
- Pretty stationery or note card boxes.
- Cookie or tea tins.
- If you're presenting someone with theater tickets, tickets to a sporting event or even a gift certificate, use a box from something you've recently gotten for yourself—an appliance, cosmetics, etc., so the contents can *really* be a surprise.

✄ Garnish the wrapped gift with a small trinket or knickknack:

- A rattle in the bow of a baby gift.
- A tree ornament on a Christmas gift.
- A small toy in the ribbon of a gift for a child.
- A small kitchen utensil on a bridal shower gift.
- Colorful, funky shoelaces hanging from a kid's present.
- Bite-size candies in colorful cellophane attached to any gift.
- A packet of seeds attached to a gardener's gift.

In conclusion

We hope that with this book as your trusty gift-giving companion you can eliminate the stress of finding just the right gift for anyone. Although gift-giving is usually associated with a celebration, gift-shopping often produces less-than-celebratory feelings. *Will this fit? Is this her color? Is this extravagant enough? Is this too extravagant? How can I get an appropriate gift on my budget?*

On and on we agonize. Throughout all this, we forget that the reason we are giving a gift is to express an important sentiment: love, like, appreciation, admiration, etc. That is the important thing, and by keeping it in mind (and using all the valuable suggestions in this book), gift-giving will never—okay, *hardly* ever—be a chore again.

And you thought catalogs were junk mail

Gift-shopping needn't require much more effort than it takes to make a toll-free call, what with the numerous direct-mail outfits reaching out to share their wares with consumers. This option is a great solution for those long-distance gift-giving occasions. You can call a mail-order company from the comfort of your easy chair—at 3 a.m. if you choose—present your credit card information, order the item and have it sent gift-wrapped to arrive at the recipient's address in as little as a few days. Some even offer next-day delivery for an additional charge.

The following is but a small sampling of the mail-order catalogs available, including some pertinent information about ordering and gift-wrapping services. Simply call and ask to be put on the mailing list, and in a short while, you'll start receiving the catalog.

Please note that, unless otherwise indicated, you should be able to reach a catalog representative 7 days a week, 24 hours a day. Also, when ordering over the phone, a major credit card is required.

General items

Miles Kimball
414-231-4886

From windsocks, bird barns and lawn aerator sandals to convenience items such as foldable shopping carts and pick-up tongs, Miles

Kimball offers a variety of inexpensive and unusual items, including lots of personalized stuff, like the 12-month, 12-photo calendar and pencils for kids. Standard delivery time is about 2 weeks. (Personalized gifts, however, will take longer.) You can guarantee delivery within 4 days for an additional $11. Gift-wrapping is not provided, but they will include a gift message at no cost. Overseas shipping is only available when billed to the same overseas address.

The Sharper Image
800-344-4444

Featured in a recent catalog are such high-tech novelties as the "world's smallest and lightest digital camcorder" for a mere $2,500. But more reasonably priced gift items are included as well—such as the audio pillow ($30) for insomniacs who can't fall asleep without a little night music. Delivery time on many items is about 4 business days, but they offer 2-day delivery for an additional charge (varies based on value of order). And they'll gift-wrap almost any product for free, or deluxe giftwrap with a personalized gift card for $6.95. Overseas delivery available on most items.

Brookstone
800-926-7000

Another great source of hard-to-find (and sometimes hard-to-imagine) gadgets. We found a facial exerciser, a window-glass vacuumer and a car grocery bag organizer. But there are a lot of practical and decorative items—and lots of outdoor and garden stuff. Most items are delivered within 5 to 7 business days, but you can request 2-day or overnight delivery for an additional cost (varies depending upon the merchandise). Gift-wrapping is $5 per package. Overseas shipping is available.

Lillian Vernon
800-285-5555

One of the most well-known mail-order services, Lillian Vernon offers a gift-packed catalog of practical, whimsical and decorative household items, holiday gifts and plenty of personalized possibilities—such as a monogrammed, gold-plated blush brush or a child's Easter basket.

Standard delivery is within 10 business days, and 4-day delivery is available for an additional $7.50. Personalized items take a day longer. No gift-wrapping provided, but they will include a gift message with the item.

Wireless
800-669-9999

"A Catalog for Fans and Friends of Public Radio" and anyone else who would appreciate a source of unique gifts—such as an aquarium that looks like a computer monitor or a mouse pad resembling a Ouija board. Also, a lot of personalized items. Standard delivery is 7 to 10 days, and overnight delivery (call before 2 p.m. CST) can be guaranteed for an additional cost (varies between $13 and $20). Gift-wrapping is $3.95 per item. Overseas shipping is available.

Signals
800-669-9696

"A Catalog for Fans and Friends of Public Television," these items are from the same source as the Wireless catalog. Same type of stuff—but not the *same* stuff. A personalized zodiac necklace caught our eye. Standard delivery is 7 to 10 days, and overnight delivery (call before 2 p.m. CST) can be guaranteed for an additional cost (varies between $13 and $20). Gift-wrapping is $3.95 per item. Overseas shipping is available.

Hold Everything
800-421-2264

This source features classy and decoratively correct household items, with an emphasis on organizing and storage items. Holiday storage boxes for ornaments and decorations, men's valets, tie and belt hangers, travel items—and an array of attractive home and office storage receptacles in rattan, wood, wire and more. Most orders arrive within 5 business days. Gifts can be wrapped for $3.25; a gift message is included at no charge. Overseas shipping is not available.

Personal

The Body Shop
800-541-2535

Personal care products from hair to toes. The wide range of products available includes peppermint foot lotion, coconut shampoo and kiwi lip balm. Gift packs are available, and there's even a pack for kids. Good to know: You can return empty bottles for recycling and be credited 5 cents. Packages (which, by the way, are shipped in reusable, biodegradable materials) arrive within 3 to 4 business days. Overnight orders cost an additional $12. Items can be basketed, bucketed or bagged for an additional $3—gift message included. Overseas shipping is only available to military addresses.

Foods and kitchenware

Harry & David
800-547-3033

Famous for their Royal Riviera Pears, locally grown in Oregon, they also have a wide range of other fruits, as well as cakes, preserves, smoked foods and more. Delivery time is about 2 weeks, possibly longer for fruits, depending on ripeness. Shipping in 3 to 5 business days is an extra $6.95, in 2 days an extra $15.95 and overnight an extra $25. Fruits may be shipped boxed or in a basket. Gift notes included at no extra charge. Overseas shipping is available on some items, but not on fruit.

Williams Sonoma
800-541-2233

Cooking supplies and gourmet foods, from syrups, preserves and salsas to yogurt makers, breadmakers and dinnerware as well as hundreds of kitchen tools and gadgets. Standard delivery time is about 7 business days. Gift-wrapping is available on some items for $3.75. Overseas shipping is not available.

Wolferman's Muffins
800-999-1910

A variety of baked goods, such as tea breads, crumpets, cinnamon rolls and, of course, muffins, is available in a range of flavors. Also available are many preserves and spreads. Gift baskets and sampler baskets are available. Standard delivery is about 7 days; overnight delivery is available for an additional $15. No gift-wrapping, but gift notes are provided at no charge. No overseas shipping.

Business/career

Day-Timers
800-225-5005
Monday-Friday, 8 a.m. to midnight ET

A great source for co-worker gifts or for friends or family focused on career. Items include, of course, the Day-Timer calendars (the bulk of the catalog is devoted to this stuff), but also business card holders, pen holders, portfolios in various styles, pen and pencil sets, even stationery, desk clocks and organizer accessories. Lots of personalized items. Standard delivery is 3 to 9 business days. Overnight costs include a $12.50 handling fee in addition to the overnight shipping charges, which vary depending on the item(s) being shipped. No gift-wrapping, except during Christmas, but they do include a gift message. Overseas shipping is available.

Wall Street Creations Ltd.
800-575-9255
Monday-Friday, 8:30 a.m. to 5:30 p.m. ET

Within the pages of this catalog are the perfect gifts for that financial planner, stockbroker and the finance-conscious. Lots of bulls-and-bears paraphernalia, desk accessories, money-themed ties, suspenders and plaques. Personalization of many items. Standard delivery within 3 to 7 business days. Overnight and 2-day delivery is available for an additional charge (varies). No gift-wrapping service, but they will enclose a card with any item. Overseas shipping is available.

Clothing

L.L. Bean
800-221-4221

Lots of great high-quality clothing along with stuff for the outdoor lover. Parkas, boots, thermal underwear, sweaters, swimwear, hiking shorts and more. Also, luggage, totes, gloves, socks, hats, pocket tools, travel items and gadgets such as headlamps. Regular delivery is pretty fast—2 to 4 days, or pay an additional $6 for next-day delivery. While there's no gift-wrapping, they will include a message at no charge. L.L. Bean also offers a gift registry service and overseas mailing.

Lands' End
800-356-4444

Featured are casual clothing, sportswear and shoes for men and women as well as luggage, duffel bags, sheets and towels. Lots of opportunities for monogramming (shirts, canvas briefcases and towels) for a mere $5 per item. Gift boxing is $5 per box. Merchandise is typically delivered in 3 business days but you can guarantee 2-day delivery (if you call by 10 a.m.) for an additional $6. (Monogramming requires additional time.) Overseas shipping is available.

Victoria's Secret
800-888-8200

The source for sexy lingerie, underwear and nightwear, this catalog also offers women's clothing for office, evening and weekend. Items usually arrive within 7 to 10 days from ordering, but you can guarantee delivery in 3 days ($5 more), 2 days ($10 more) or overnight ($15 more). For $2, you will receive a gift-wrap kit with the merchandise you order, or you can have the item wrapped for $8. A gift message is free of charge. Overseas shipping is available.

Travel items

Travelsmith
800-950-1600
Monday-Friday, 5 a.m. to 8 p.m., Saturday, Sunday, 8 a.m. to 4 p.m. ET

This catalog offers everything for the travel *aficionado* including lots of luggage possibilities, travel-friendly clothing and unique items such as a bomb-proof glasses case and official Swiss army socks. All orders are same-day shipped (delivery within 2 to 10 working days) and over-night delivery can be guaranteed for an extra $12. There is no gift-wrapping, but you can include a note at no extra charge. Overseas shipping is available.

Orvis
800-541-3541

Another excellent source of travel gear, sports equipment and sportswear—from a rolling golf club case for those who can't go any-where without a nine-iron to a highway emergency kit. There are also specific catalogs for fly-fishing, hunting, travel and women's wear. Delivery is within 3 to 10 business days; next-day delivery can be guar-anteed for $15. Gift-wrapping is $4.95. Overseas shipping is available.

Children's

The Disney Catalog
800-237-5751

A perfect source for children's gifts, this catalog includes colorful kids' clothing and lots and lots of toys—such as Mickey Mouse watches, Cinderella music boxes, Esmeralda costumes and a whole cast of famil-iar figurines and dolls, including Goofy, Donald Duck, Beauty and the Beast, Quasimodo and more. The catalog even carries clothes for grown-ups. Orders delivered within 4 to 8 business days, and 2-day delivery guaranteed for $15. Gift boxes are $5.50 each; gift messages are free. Overseas shipping is available.

Sports

Eastbay
800-826-2205

Featured are shoes for any athletic occasion, sports uniforms, fitness wear and sports equipment—as well as replica jerseys of America's favorite sports teams. Also available are sports totes, shoulder bags and backpacks, portable cassette and CD players. Standard delivery within 4 to 6 business days, and overnight delivery guaranteed for $21.99 extra. No gift-wrapping or message cards included. Overseas shipping is available.

The bizarre

Johnson Smith Co.
941-747-2356
Monday-Friday, 8 a.m. to 5 p.m. ET

The source for some of the more unusual gift suggestions listed in this book (the place to order your personalized face gelatin mold, for example), this catalog claims to offer a range of "things you never knew existed—and other items you can't possibly live without." Once you learn that glowing-skull boxer shorts or a boxing nun hand puppet are available, you won't be able to live without this resource. Standard delivery is within 2 weeks. Pay an additional $2.95 for guaranteed 4- to 5-day delivery. Gift-wrapping is $2.95 per package, and they charge $3.50 for any package shipped to a different address from the one billed. Overseas shipping is available.

Give 'em a call: Other numbers throughout the book

So, you forgot where you saw that phone number we gave you for ordering a really great gift? Luckily, we have listed these numbers for you again by chapter here.

Please note that phone numbers, store names and especially prices may change.

Mentioned in Chapter 2

American Association of Retired Persons (p. 24): 800-424-3410

Bath of the Month Club (p. 35): 800-406-2284

Beer Across America (p. 31): 800-854-2337

Flowers (p. 26): 800-836-PETAL

Library of Congress (*Choice Magazine Listening*) (p. 26): 516-883-8280

Poland Spring (p. 21): 800-759-9251

Transmedia (p. 23): 800-422-5090

Mentioned in Chapter 3

International Star Registry, The (p. 56): 800-282-3333

International Wildlife Coalition (IWC) (p. 57): 508-548-8328

Mentioned in Chapter 5

Boxers of the Month Club (p. 78): 800-746-7875

International Wine Cellars (p. 77): 800-854-2337

Wine Hobby (p. 74): 800-847-HOPS

Mentioned in Chapter 6

Croll Clocks (p. 90): 201-484-5781

Mentioned in Chapter 7

Coffee Quest (p. 115): 800-854-2337

Tender Loving Things, Inc. (p. 119): 800-486-2896

Mentioned in Chapter 8

Back to the 50s (p. 136): 800-224-1950

Desperate Enterprises, Inc. (p. 125): 216-732-4859

Ott's (discount art supplies) (p. 127): 800-356-3289

Rick's Movie Graphics (p. 128): 800-252-0425

U.S. Mint (p. 124): 202-283-COIN

U.S. Postal Service (p. 124): 800-STAMP-24

Gift-giving organizers

D o you need a place to record important occasions now that you have some exciting gift ideas for them? You can purchase a notebook or other premade booklet to keep track of important dates, or you can start your list right here. Just turn to each month and fill in who, what, when and why for every gift-giving occasion! Included here are:

- **12 months of gift calendar sheets.** Fill in names, dates and the occasion so when it's time to get a gift, you'll know ahead of time...if you look at the sheets, that is.

- **Gift profile sheets.** One place for all important gift-buying information. Name, size, favorite color...and more.

- **A gift history sheet.** Remember the woman in the beginning of the book who turned around and gave the same gift to someone that the person had given to her the year before? Well, this list will help you avoid that type of embarrassment.

Make sure you make photocopies of these sheets before you write on them so that you'll have extras you can use again and again.

January

Person_____

Date_____

Occasion_____

Person_____

Date_____

Occasion_____

Person_____

Date_____

Occasion_____

Person_____

Date_____

Occasion_____

Person_____

Date_____

Occasion_____

Person_____

Date_____

Occasion_____

February

Person_____

Date_____

Occasion_____

Person_____

Date_____

Occasion_____

Person_____

Date_____

Occasion_____

Person_____

Date_____

Occasion_____

Person_____

Date_____

Occasion_____

Person_____

Date_____

Occasion_____

March

Person_____

Date_____

Occasion_____

Person_____

Date_____

Occasion_____

Person_____

Date_____

Occasion_____

Person_____

Date_____

Occasion_____

Person_____

Date_____

Occasion_____

Person_____

Date_____

Occasion_____

April

Person_____

Date_____

Occasion_____

Person_____

Date_____

Occasion_____

Person_____

Date_____

Occasion_____

Person_____

Date_____

Occasion_____

Person_____

Date_____

Occasion_____

Person_____

Date_____

Occasion_____

May

Person_____

Date_____

Occasion_____

Person_____

Date_____

Occasion_____

Person_____

Date_____

Occasion_____

Person_____

Date_____

Occasion_____

Person_____

Date_____

Occasion_____

Person_____

Date_____

Occasion_____

June

Person_____

Date_____

Occasion_____

Person_____

Date_____

Occasion_____

Person_____

Date_____

Occasion_____

Person_____

Date_____

Occasion_____

Person_____

Date_____

Occasion_____

Person_____

Date_____

Occasion_____

July

Person_____

Date_____

Occasion_____

Person_____

Date_____

Occasion_____

Person_____

Date_____

Occasion_____

Person_____

Date_____

Occasion_____

Person_____

Date_____

Occasion_____

Person_____

Date_____

Occasion_____

August

Person_____

Date_____

Occasion_____

Person_____

Date_____

Occasion_____

Person_____

Date_____

Occasion_____

Person_____

Date_____

Occasion_____

Person_____

Date_____

Occasion_____

Person_____

Date_____

Occasion_____

September

Person_____

Date_____

Occasion_____

Person_____

Date_____

Occasion_____

Person_____

Date_____

Occasion_____

Person_____

Date_____

Occasion_____

Person_____

Date_____

Occasion_____

Person_____

Date_____

Occasion_____

October

Person_____

Date_____

Occasion_____

Person_____

Date_____

Occasion_____

Person_____

Date_____

Occasion_____

Person_____

Date_____

Occasion_____

Person_____

Date_____

Occasion_____

Person_____

Date_____

Occasion_____

November

Person_____

Date_____

Occasion_____

Person_____

Date_____

Occasion_____

Person_____

Date_____

Occasion_____

Person_____

Date_____

Occasion_____

Person_____

Date_____

Occasion_____

Person_____

Date_____

Occasion_____

December

Person_____

Date_____

Occasion_____

Person_____

Date_____

Occasion_____

Person_____

Date_____

Occasion_____

Person_____

Date_____

Occasion_____

Person_____

Date_____

Occasion_____

Person_____

Date_____

Occasion_____

Gift Profile

Name_____

Address_____

Birthdate_____Anniversary_____

Key clothing sizes_____

_____

_____

_____

_____

Ring size_____

Birthstone_____

Pierced ears? Yes_____ No_____

Favorite color(s)_____

_____

Favorite scent_____

Favorite foods_____

_____

Favorite flower_____

Career/job_____

Favorite hobbies/interests_____

_____

_____

_____

_____

Allergies/dislikes_____

_____

Gift Profile

Name_____

Address_____

Birthdate_____Anniversary_____

Key clothing sizes_____

_____

_____

_____

_____

Ring size_____

Birthstone_____

Pierced ears? Yes_____ No_____

Favorite color(s)_____

_____

Favorite scent_____

Favorite foods_____

_____

Favorite flower_____

Career/job_____

Favorite hobbies/interests_____

_____

_____

_____

_____

Allergies/dislikes_____

_____

Gift History

Date	Occasion	Item	Reaction

Send us your ideas!!

If you've got a few great gift ideas of your own or know of some catalogs you think would be of benefit to readers, we'd like to hear from you! Just fill in the form below and mail it to: Career Press, Inc., Editorial Dept., 3 Tice Rd., P.O. Box 687, Franklin Lakes, NJ 07417. We'll consider your suggestions for the next edition of *1,001 Great Gifts*.

Name:_____

Address:_____

_____

Phone:_____

Gift ideas for the next edition of *1,001 Great Gifts*:

_____

_____

_____

_____

_____

_____

_____

_____

Mail-order companies, catalogs and other sources of great gifts:

_____

_____

_____

_____

_____

_____

_____